ADVANCE PRAISE

I commend Ms. Ruth Lature for her passion and drive to help dyslexic children and adults and for her work to educate others about the challenges inherent in this neurological disorder. Her experiences remind me of my childhood when my fourth-grade teacher recognized that I was struggling with dyslexia. Receiving the assistance I needed changed my life and opened the world of reading to me. I am pleased that Mississippi has taken steps to aid dyslexic students and strengthen therapy opportunities.

—Phil Bryant, Governor of Mississippi

Teachers and parents of dyslexic children will welcome this intriguing memoir of how intensive multisensory language training transformed Ms. Lature's life both personally and professionally.

—Marcia Henry, Ph.D., Professor Emerita, San Jose State University; past president, International Dyslexia Association; author, *Unlocking Literacy: Effective Decoding and Spelling Instruction*

Ruth Lature has been helping people with dyslexia for over forty-two years. In this memoir, "Dyslexia: A Teacher's Journey," Ruth reminds us that dyslexia occurs in people of all backgrounds and intellectual levels, that it is not a psychological disorder, that it is a learning disability, and that it prevents people from fulfilling their potential. We have an opportunity to transform the diagnosis, understanding, and treatment of dyslexia and this book can help lead the way. Thanks to Ruth and her fellow professionals for their leadership, dedication and commitment.

—Ed Whitfield, representative U. S. Congress

Ruth Lature's book, "Dyslexia: A Teachers Journey," touches my heart and revives memories of my similar journey. In a small city in Mississippi, I heard of the work of Dr. Charles Shedd. He generously traveled to our community and trained us to help hundreds of children. He was the most dedicated person I have ever known. I admired him and was grateful for his genius and devotion. In telling the story of her experiences in developing lasting programs in Kentucky, Ruth shares the struggle to educate students, parents, educators, and legislators to the reality of dyslexia and the toll it takes on those who, though intelligent, struggle to learn to read, write, and spell.

—Joyce S. Pickering, Hum. D., Executive Director Emerita, Shelton School & Evaluation Center, Dallas, Texas

Dyslexia
A TEACHER'S JOURNEY

A Memoir

RUTH FULLER LATURE

DYSLEXIA: A TEACHER'S JOURNEY

This book is manufactured in the United States of America.

Publisher:
Darby Press, LLC
Louisville, Kentucky 40204

ISBN   978-0-9834144-5-2
Soft cover
First Edition

Library of Congress Number 2013936428

Lature, Ruth
Dyslexia: A Teacher's Journey

Interior Layout, Editor
Peggy DeKay, peggy@tbowt. com
http://tbowt. com

Contact the author at lature1445@aol.com
Author website: www.ruthlature.com

A percentage of the net proceeds from the sale of this book will be donated to organizations which support education and advocacy for persons with dyslexia.

DISCLAIMER

Dyslexia: A Teacher's Journey is creative non-fiction written by an educator who worked with and advocated for persons with dyslexia for forty-two years. In order to preserve confidentiality, identifying facts have been changed. Time fades memory and blunts feelings, but bolstered by notes kept by Lature through the years, the battles and triumphs in this book are based on her experiences.

This book is dedicated to my late husband, James William Lature, who gave me the freedom to pursue my passion.

Contents

PART TWO: HOME

FOREWORD

Despite having known and been associated with Ruth in a number of ways for many years, it was not until I became a board member of the Dyslexia Association of the Pennyrile, Hopkinsville, Kentucky, that I truly saw Ruth as the determined, pioneering person for specific learning disabilities. Whether it is screening, teaching persons with specific learning disabilities to read, serving on and guiding the local dyslexia board, or "bird-dogging" legislators, she is Ms. Dyslexia of the Pennyrile and Kentucky.

She developed her passion for persons with specific reading/learning disabilities many years ago and set about in a very methodical, determined manner to educate and equip herself to teach and to raise dyslexia awareness in schools and in our community helping to eliminate the stigma of "dummy" most frequently associated with the dyslexic.

John H. Freer, MD

ACKNOWLEDGEMENT

I extend my heartfelt thanks to the named and unnamed persons who have helped me nurture this book to maturity. Had it not been for eighty-nine-year-old Michael Freeland's restarting of the Hoptown Writers Group, this unfinished manuscript probably would still be on a shelf. Thanks to Michael and to the group for inspiring, motivating, and advising.

Thanks to my advisors and proofreaders: Joan Harris, "the sister I never had," Warren Sully, my immensely considerate and caring friend, and to Betty Grogan, my talented neighbor.

Last but certainly not least, my book coach, Peggy DeKay, Louisville, Kentucky, whose ideas, advice, and criticism kept me headed in the right direction and who walked me through the editing, publishing, and promotional process.

INTRODUCTION

Several years ago, a fifteen-year-old boy wrote:

"I'm dyslexic. I have been screwed up in school. I'm thinking about running away because school is too much for me, If I had good grades, I would have friends that I could hang around with and not get in trouble. The only friends I have is [sic] trouble makers and I am one of them. I have been to court twice. The first time was for shooting cars, the second time was assault and battery me and another guy...."[sic]

This statement could have been written today. Progress has come far too slowly.

More recently Maria, a fifty-three–year-old woman drove into our screening site accompanied by her mother. She had a screening appointment with our psychologist. Maria had seen a public-service announcement on television about dyslexia.

For the first time in her life, she understood that a disorder called "dyslexia" existed and felt it could be at the heart of her life-long problem. Maria had never held a job outside the home. She had few friends and was dependent on her elderly mother.

Following the screening and a diagnosis of dyslexia, this affable and unpretentious woman sat across from me and told her story, her face drenched in tears. She had hidden her inability to read from her husband. Only her mother knew.

"You cannot imagine the stress I have been under all my life to hide my inability to read. In Sunday school I was miserable—afraid they would ask me to read. I can't even read the Bible," she said.

As I kept handing her tissues, she continued, "You will never know what it means to find out I am not the only one with this affliction and that it even has a name."

When I explained to her that dyslexic persons are intelligent and can learn to read—that they just need to be taught differently—she was elated. "You mean there is hope for me? Oh, if only I could read and not be haunted by the excruciating fear of being humiliated!"

Determined to keep her secret, we arranged for one of our highly trained tutors, Mrs. Stanley, who had worked in our tutorial program for many years, to see her at the tutor's home. Mrs. Stanley was a take-charge woman with a deep passion for people in pain. She worked patiently with Maria twice a week for one year. Maria began to read, write, and spell, increasing her skills by two grade levels.

With many severely dyslexic adults, progress comes slowly and even the most exuberant individuals waver in dedication to their goal. In some older students, the brain has lost some of its plasticity, making it more difficult for them to learn.

We helped Maria acquire new reading skills. As she became more confident, her self-worth increased and she no longer felt a need to harbor that dark secret inside her.

A highly reputable psychologist referred a fifty-year-old man diagnosed with dyslexia. Sampson, although highly intelligent, had labored in the coal mines of western Kentucky until he was injured in an underground cave-in. Now suffering a crippling physical disability from which he would never completely recover, he was even more distraught over his inability to read.

His school had done nothing to help him.

"Oh, yes, they did one thing," he said. "When I was in the ninth grade, they sent me back to read with first-graders."

Dyslexia imprisons and it is not always behind metal bars.

Dr. Charles L. Shedd, psychologist and researcher on dyslexia, had been conducting a Reading Research Institute at Berea College, Berea, Kentucky, for ten years. Students with dyslexia from five to twenty-one years old came from the southeastern part of the United States. At the same time, Dr. Shedd chose persons with potential to work at the institute and to go back to their communities and use the knowledge acquired to start low-cost, effective programs. Colleges were not teaching educators how to deal with dyslexia in public education. I was excited to be chosen.

PART ONE

SUMMER OF 1970

Chapter 1
The Reading Research Institute

I wondered why somebody didn't do something; then I realized that I was somebody.

—Anonymous

After several hours of driving, I arrived at Berea College in Berea, Kentucky. A man dressed in cut-off jeans and a dingy white shirt, which he used to wipe sweat from his brow, directed me to a small wooden building. The heat of many summers had long since burned the paint from the wooden dorm. The wood, turned to silver gray, made the building look tired. Rain had given the tin roof patches of rust.

Berea College had a tradition dating from 1859 of helping students with great promise and limited economic resources. With a unique labor program, Berea was a place students gained work experience and a tuition-free college education while developing a sense of community and concern for others. What a fitting place to learn a low-cost type of remediation for persons with dyslexia, which had formerly been available on a limited basis only to the more affluent.

My Roommate

As I carefully climbed the broken steps into the main room, I noticed the wooden floor strewn with well-worn, scattered rugs. Old chairs and sofas with faded covers were dispersed around the room. Checking in, I soon met my roommate, a graceful white-haired teacher, Frances Crocker, from Alabama.

Frances was an elementary teacher who had done private tutoring with persons with dyslexia. She, like me, felt unprepared to take on such an awesome responsibility. Both of us had felt the pain and had witnessed the plight of this devastating, invisible, disability called dyslexia.

Although Frances was considerably older than I, we quickly formed a close bond. Frances had no children and had recently lost her husband to melanoma. "A seemingly harmless dark raised area appeared on his thigh," she said with trembling voice. "By the time I could get him to an oncologist, the cancer could not be controlled," she managed to say.

To keep from losing her composure, she shifted the conversation. "I am disappointed with our living conditions. This dormitory must be a left over from the founding of the college in the mid-1880s." Lying propped up on her twin bed with an iron headboard that had peeling white paint, Frances continued, "There is no air-conditioning and we share a community bathroom down the hall. There is no hot water, so I guess our cold shower in the morning will keep us cool for the day."

I thought to myself, *If our students live a lifetime with dyslexia, I suppose we can survive this for nine weeks.*

Our First Assembly

As the staff of the Reading Institute for Students with Dyslexia assembled in the downstairs meeting room that evening with Dr. Shedd, the director, I was excited to participate in this work-to-learn program.

I had met Dr. Shedd when he came to my hometown to speak the previous fall. Like the nearly three-hundred desperate parents, teachers, and community leaders who assembled in the First United Methodist Church, I listened to Dr. Shedd speak passionately and boldly about dyslexia. His wealth of information from experience, research, and vicariously "walking in the shoes" of a dyslexic jolted those who heard him out of their complacency. He did not hesitate to challenge prevailing thought to dispel the ignorance that surrounded dyslexia.

Now at Berea, Dr. Shedd's quick brown eyes darted from person to person. They observed the zest in his step and sensed his unyielding drive. Cool air swirled from the ceiling fans. Dressed in a plaid shirt and jeans, he seated himself on a tattered rug and leaned against the plastered wall. With his agility and small stature, he seemed to have found the perfect settee. Had I not met him previously, I might have mistaken him for the janitor. The group became quiet and attentive. Dr. Shedd spoke briefly but with urgency, hope, and vision.

My self-confidence began to wane and insecurity overtook me as he outlined his expectations. I felt boxed-in. What had I gotten into? Dr. Shedd was expecting far more of me than I had imagined. Would I humiliate myself and cheat the students with my mediocrity? Where was the exuberance I experienced only moments ago?

I slept little that night—not because of the lumpy bed, the sweltering hot room, or my looming feelings of inadequacy but from renewed excitement. I had the opportunity that my master's degree from one of the top teacher-training institutions had not given me. I was finally going to learn how to help the Toms of this world. As I drifted between wakefulness and sleep, I thought about Tom.

Tom, in the Beginning

In the fall of 1967, my school system opened a reading clinic. During that summer, I survived competition throughout the United States to win the opportunity to attend an eight-week government-funded reading institute at George Peabody College for Teachers in Nashville, Tennessee. I met the word *dyslexia*, for the first time that summer. However, we did not become acquainted, for instruction focused on reading in general. Because I was an attendee at this summer-long workshop, school supervisors thought I was a good choice to work at the reading clinic. That's where I met Tom.

Tom came for testing upon the recommendation of his teachers. A social worker brought Tom to the clinic and introduced him.

He was of medium height and a little chubby in the abdomen. His knit shirt barely covered his stomach. He was dressed in freshly ironed and creased jeans. His short-cropped hair seemed to cling to the top of his head.

I pointed to a chair close to my desk and said, "Good morning, Tom, you may have a seat here. I have a few activities we are going to do together to try to find out how we can better help you with your reading."

In a subdued voice, Tom replied, "Okay," and I saw a hint of a smile on his face.

Slow to move, he quietly seated himself. He seemed oblivious to the chatter and banging in the hallway and he rarely made eye contact, often staring at his hands. By following my instructions, I could tell he was listening intently. Below is some of the astonishing information I discovered through individual testing.

Tom was fourteen years old and in grade seven and had an intelligence quotient of ninety on the

Peabody Picture Vocabulary Test[1], which is in the average range. Out of one hundred twelve Dolch[2] Basic Sight Words, he could read *I, black, look*. Even though Tom appeared to look at each word carefully, he could not read such words as *by, at, do, his, get.*

On a diagnostic spelling test, Tom could spell **none** of the words correctly. The test contained such words as *not, gut, get, sit.* Amazingly, Tom was persistent as he wrote something for each of the thirty-two words, even though what he wrote generally had little resemblance to the correct word. Tom could name fifteen of the uppercase letters and thirteen of the lowercase letters. He could make none of the consonant sounds. As Tom began to twist in his seat, I showed him where the restroom was located. Then I offered him a package of cheese and crackers and a bottle of water. While Tom ate, we talked — or at least I did.

"Tom, you are a smart young man; but for some unknown reason, you find it harder to learn to read than most people." I attempted to boost his flagging self-esteem by helping him understand his condition.

He nodded his drooped head and said, "Yes'm," as he placed the wrapper from his cheese and crackers in the wastepaper basket.

I took a sip of my coffee and remarked, "I bet there are things you are good at that I am not. Do you play sports?"

Finally, Tom opened up. "Play football...." His dynamics abruptly changed and I thought Tom would never stop talking about football so we could get back to work!

I noticed a few reversals such as *b/d, m/n,* which the public commonly associates with dyslexia. Tom could comprehend paragraphs when read to him, but he could not comprehend silently because he did not recognize the words.

Tom's Parents

A few days later, I made a visit to his home. He lived in an urban neighborhood that had seen better days. I parked my white Mustang on peeling asphalt near the grassy yard that was beginning to brown. Far in the distance, I heard barking dogs. Walking to the door, I took in the enticing smell of grilling hamburgers.

Mrs. Stone answered my knock on the door. Even though Tom's parents were expecting me, I introduced myself. Mrs. Stone was tall and slender, with shoulders beginning to stoop. Her short black hair had a few specks of gray, reminding me that she was older than most of the parents whose children I taught.

As I entered the room, Mr. Stone rose from a reclining chair and came forward to shake hands. Both parents were gentle, kind people who warmly welcomed me into their impeccably tidy home. Mrs. Stone offered tea or coffee. The smell of freshly brewed coffee lured me to accept her offer. Then we settled down to a serious discussion concerning Tom's reading.

Tom's mother said, "Tom's brothers and sisters have learned to read with ease. Maybe I should have worked with Tom more. Maybe that fall that I had when carrying Tom did something to him."

"Just as some people are born with black hair and some with brown, some people are born finding it more difficult to learn to read than others. Nothing you did or didn't do had anything to do with Tom's reading problem." If I accomplished nothing else, I wanted to alleviate her guilt.

The father was quiet. However, his presence expressed his intense interest in his son. It was difficult to get fathers to come to school for conferences, and most had skipped the few at-home appointments I made as a young teacher.

Tom's father talked about his work as a farm hand. "When the weather breaks in the spring, I work from daylight to dark on Mr. Soyars' farm until the crops are all in. Then I sit day after day stripping tobacco. I want my family to have a better life than this."

These humble, concerned parents thanked me profusely for my interest. I left knowing I had their full cooperation in whatever I thought best for Tom. I was glad we had this talk. The chilling air that engulfed me as I climbed back into my car brought despair as I questioned myself. *What was best for Tom? Did I have the knowledge and skills to help him?*

In my report to his school, I suggested that Tom be referred to a local psychologist for a specific diagnosis. My other suggestion was that "he be made to feel accepted and helped to form a positive self-concept." How could he have a positive self-concept, though, when he was in the seventh grade and a non-reader?

After testing at a local mental-health center, the psychologist wrote in January 1968: "While it is impossible to rule out a perceptual handicap or brain damage at this time, the results obtained today would not support such a hypothesis. He is a friendly, personable and cooperative boy with average ability who appears to be willing to put forth his best efforts."

Her conclusion—no psychological disorder found. The psychological evaluation was worthless.

Tom after Berea

After training at Berea College and returning home, I taught Tom until 1971. At that time, my final report to the school stated: "We have been using a teaching method unavailable until this year. Tom has made more progress this year than in the previous two years combined. Achievement tests show him to be reading at 1.9, or nearly second-grade level."

Though improved, Tom was still reading on a pathetically low level. I wish I could have seen him daily rather than once a week. Still, his progress was good for a severe dyslexic his age. I went on to say in my report:

> *How Tom has performed in school sufficiently to reach the tenth-grade level is beyond my comprehension. Tom tries so hard and has a positive attitude toward reading and everyone involved. However, I am sure Tom has some type of reading disability that even psychologists have been unable to define.* (In fact, I thought he was dyslexic, but I could not say that. I was only a teacher.)

On a Tuesday morning, Tom burst into my office at the reading clinic without knocking and rushed toward me waving a card in my face. My suspicion quieted my resistance to this rambunctious, atypical behavior.

"I just passed my driver's license test!" Tom yelled. This was a crowning moment in both our lives. I had recorded the study manual. Tom had listened to the tape until he knew the information. The examiner administered the test orally. An ecstatic young man left my room as I prayed silently, *Oh, God, please help Tom read the traffic signs.*

Chapter 2
Day One at Berea

If you think you are too small to make a difference, try sleeping with a mosquito.

—Dalai Lama

Ring, ring, ring—the alarm sounded. I reached to turn it off as Frances opened her eyes. Feather-like fresh air from the open window brushed my skin and helped my mind become fully conscious. Out of bed, I gathered towel, washcloth, soap, and shower cap then, squeezed between her bed and mine mumbling, "I'm headed for the shower."

The cool water was invigorating but did nothing to erase the anxiety of my new surroundings. As I left the bathroom, Frances and I passed in the hall and managed to smile. Doors began to open and muffled female voices could be heard in the hall.

Francis and I dressed hurriedly, each taking our turn at the tiny room mirror. Notebook in hand, we carefully made our way down squeaky stairs. Frances volunteered, "There should be a railing on at least one side. A fifty-two-year-old lady could easily take a tumble." I agreed. The stairs appeared minutes away from collapsing.

As we headed for breakfast, Connie and Trina caught up with us. "Can you believe that Carrie drove from Florida to work in this program, surveyed our living conditions, and is already headed back to Florida? 'I am not living in this dump,' she told me."

I was stunned that anyone would be that discouraged over less than ideal living conditions. I had never been accustomed to affluence, and my parents still did not have air-conditioning. I grew up in a four-room farmhouse. Two of the rooms were average size, but the other two were half-size. My grandmother lived in two of the four rooms. My parents and I, along with my brother, lived in the other two rooms until I went away to college.

Our toilet was a two-hole outhouse and my bathtub was a galvanized tub Mother used for laundry. We grew vegetables, raised chickens for meat and eggs, and let two pigs grow into hogs, which my dad with the help of the neighbors killed in early winter and preserved. We had plenty of homegrown food. In those days, a bologna sandwich was a big Sunday treat.

My brother and I walked over a mile on a dirt road in rain, sleet, or snow to ride a bus to school. I never missed a day of school because of weather. On at least one occasion, I crawled across a slick, ice-covered bridge without railings. I feared sliding into the icy water below.

At the bus stop, there was a grocery store with a vacant building adjacent to it. The owners let us stash our muddy overshoes and extra coats there during the school day. We didn't need those extra farm coats once we got on the warm bus. I can still imagine the dreadful looks and hear the whispers of other students had we gotten on the bus wearing the wet and muddy overshoes. Overshoes worn over school shoes kept mud from spreading in the bus and buildings.

I thought I was different from others, and I suppose I was at the time. I realize that this humbling experience helps me appreciate what I have today. How can we fully enjoy the mountaintop unless we have been in the valley?

The door to the red brick cafeteria jolted me back to the real world as it slammed behind me. It was one of the newest buildings on campus. Inside, the decorations were sparse, but the serving area was glistening clean. The aroma of sizzling hickory-smoked bacon, scrambled eggs, and steaming oatmeal made me ravenously hungry. The food was cooked to perfection. What a drastic contrast to our mediocre sleeping facilities. On the other hand, something was missing—no pancakes, toast and jelly, or muffins.

Sister Marie, one of Dr. Shedd's experienced staff members, sat across the table from us, so I asked, "Why no bread or even sugar for the oatmeal?"

"Our students have attention and concentration problems. Refined carbohydrates such as cookies, muffins, fruit sweetened with sugar, and sugar-coated cereal can shorten their attention span."

I was intrigued. Little did I know that Dr. Shedd was twenty years ahead of others in researching the relationship between diet and attention.

Although small, the cafeteria was not crowded. The Reading Institute staff were the only patrons at 6:45 a.m. We finished eating quickly and quietly so we would not be late for our long day of training.

In the evening, I found myself back in the cafeteria, in the same seat, feeling too depleted and overwhelmed to care about eating. What a day. We had listened intently for hours with few breaks as Dr. Shedd and his staff taught me more about the structure of language than I had learned from my entire undergraduate major in English or my masters in elementary education. From sound/symbol to phonology[3] to syllables to syntax[4] to morphology[5], Dr. Shedd taught about aspects of the language which had eluded me. Little wonder, I suppose, for I had learned to read by the look-say method. [6]

As I attempted to eat, my thoughts wandered back to undergraduate school. As I was preparing to become a teacher, I thought something was wrong with me. I might have suspected dyslexia if that word had been in my vocabulary then. My campus advisor suggested I talk to the speech professor.

Dr. Paul Moore was a rather tall person with a middle-age spread who dressed casually. His brilliant mind made up for his lack of charisma.

"Dr. Moore, I think something is wrong with me. Other students in my reading classes seem to know something I don't know," I blurted as I felt his stare. "I wonder if I should go into teaching."

Dr. Moore asked me to explain.

"I have trouble making the sounds of the letters, especially vowels. I stumble over words that others seem to pronounce with ease." These problems were heavy on my heart as I sat in front of Dr. Moore.

After a short testing/working session, he swiftly dismissed me, declaring: "There is nothing wrong with your speech. No one taught you the sounds. You learned to read by sight."

My teacher taught me to look at a word and remember it the next time I saw it—the look-say method or the whole-word approach. Today, we know that is the worst possible method of teaching a person with dyslexia. It had messed me up, too, and I was not dyslexic.

Embarrassing as it was in my first year of teaching, excellent readers in the seventh grade taught me the short vowel sounds. I felt dumb in front of my students—ignorant of something so elementary. *Is this how a person with dyslexia feels—every day? Why had I not been taught somewhere in my educational career what Dr. Shedd imparted in one day?*

How many experienced reading teachers knew a fraction of what he was teaching us? All teachers needed Dr. Shedd's information. Today for example, I am appalled when my students tell me they have never heard of the *tch* spelling rule. (When a short vowel comes before /ch/ we place a silent *t* before /ch/ except in *rich, which, such,* and *much.*)

We heard a loud crash from the back of the room. All heads turned in that direction. A young student, arriving early with his parents, had tripped and dropped his tray. As he slumped to pick the dumped contents off the floor, the tears started to flow. Oh, those fine and gross motor problems associated with dyslexia were demons. The incident interrupted my thoughts, but I shifted back to quietly processing the day.

Dr. Shedd, like a maple tree full of sap, had poured the characteristics of dyslexia into us. He wasted no time in filling our buckets to the brim as we strained to catch each drop. He had arrived at these characteristics initially through extensive research at LaGrange and Eddyville, both prisons in Kentucky, where he found seventy-percent of the population to have reading problems. Following that project, he organized and directed a teaching/research institute at Berea College for ten years.

Chapter 3
Dyslexia Is ...

Failure in school does not mean failure in life.

— Stephen Cannell, author, producer, dyslexic

While I do not intend for this book to be a discourse on what dyslexia is or is not, I would be remiss if I did not include a working definition.

Definition

The *dys* in *dyslexia* is a medical prefix meaning *difficulty* while *lexia* is a suffix meaning *reading*.

According to the International Dyslexia Association (IDA), dyslexia is:

> *A specific learning disability that is neurological in origin. It is characterized by difficulties with accurate and/or fluent word recognition and by poor spelling and decoding abilities. The difficulties typically result from a deficit in the phonological component of language that is often*

unexpected in relation to other cognitive abilities and the provision of effective classroom instruction. Secondary consequences may include problems in reading comprehension and reduced reading experience that can impede growth of vocabulary and background knowledge.[7]

The IDA Board of Directors adopted this definition on Nov. 12, 2002. The National Institute of Child Health and Human Development also concurs with this definition.

What does this definition mean? *Neurological* means that dyslexia has to do with the brain and central nervous system. Dyslexia is usually inherited but can skip generations. The phonological difficulty involves hearing the sounds and detecting the difference between one sound and another.

If a dyslexic person cannot read the words, that person will have difficulty comprehending what he is attempting to read. To some extent, vocabulary and background knowledge are acquired through reading. If reading ability is hampered, then acquisition of knowledge is impeded.

While dyslexia is often inherited, family members who exhibit similar reading problems should not feel a sense of guilt because their children have dyslexia. We do not have control over genetics. The child with dyslexia may not have inherited the problem from a parent. Dyslexia can skip generations. Rather than deny the problem exists, isn't the crucial factor to seek effective teaching methods to overcome this invisible disability early in the child's life?

I feel we can best understand dyslexia by discussing the characteristics. The purpose of this book is not to guide anyone through the teaching process.

Occasionally, I get a phone call from a teacher who says she has a student in her classroom who has dyslexia. The teacher wants a quick course over the phone. This isn't realistic. If the dyslexia is moderate to severe, the classroom teacher alone cannot correct the student's disability. The training required is far more extensive than an over-the-phone tutorial.

Dr. Shedd repeatedly said, "The greatest single indicator of dyslexia is immaturity." In light of current research, I wonder if he would make the same statement today. We may use this in suspecting dyslexia. Some children just mature more rapidly than others and we do not all enter school at the same chronological age either. The dilemma is how long to wait on this maturity factor.

My advice to parents: if you are concerned that your child may have dyslexia, have your child screened or evaluated. Choose carefully your diagnostician. Today, many school psychologists do not even acknowledge that dyslexia exists. Some diagnosticians are able to diagnose dyslexia at an earlier age than others.

In 2008, I tangled with some educators and legislators over how early dyslexia could be diagnosed. Finally, I e-mailed Dr. Lee Epstein of Louisville, Kentucky, one of the finest psychologists I have ever met, and asked him that question. Here is his answer: "Thank goodness for people like you. Dyslexia can be diagnosed in kindergarten or preschool. I would be happy to help you in pursuit of this issue."

In fact, while finishing this manuscript, I read an article from Malaysia, where, educators are developing programs for early detection in nurseries.[8]

When parents ask me whether they should get their child screened or evaluated for dyslexia, I ask another key question: In comparison with other children in the classroom, to what degree is your child showing the characteristics? The teacher should be able to answer that question. For older students, can the child comprehend significantly better when someone reads a passage to him than when he reads it silently?

We as adults reverse a letter or number and say, "Oh, I must be dyslexic." This is often done in jest, to make light of a mistake. I recall being in my physician's office at the same time as an elementary principal. He asked, "What are you doing here? Have you caught dyslexia?" Of course, dyslexia cannot be caught. That was his idea of a joke. From time to time, it is common for everyone to make a "dyslexic slip."

For the most part, characteristics discussed below are the ones Dr. Shedd taught us at Berea. Other researchers have validated these characteristics over a period of years. The list is in no particular order and is not intended to be exhaustive. Parents will not see all these characteristics. Some characteristics are observed only through highly sophisticated tests.

Dyslexia Characteristics

- **Poor spatial orientation**: One indication is losing one's place in reading. For this student, have him smoothly slide the index finger of the dominate hand directly under what he is reading. There must be a smooth movement of the finger because a dyslexic person tends to read to the rhythm of the finger. Our goal is to have him read fluently. Fluency fosters comprehension/meaning, the purpose of all reading. He can handle cursive writing better than printing. In printing, he fails to leave space between words.

- **Lack of dominance**: Some students can use either hand equally well. They might throw a ball with one hand and write with the other. Do not let students switch hands. If students tend to use the left hand, see that they always do that. On the other hand, if students prefer the right hand, make sure they consistently use it. If there is no hand preference, go with the right hand because we live in a right-handed world.

- **Directional confusion**: Dyslexic persons are often lost. When told to turn left, they are likely to turn right. Imagine the frustration to a child who is in competitive sports. A mother recently told me her son played ball but he put a big "X" on his left thigh so he could tell left from right—one clever way of coping. Other abstract concepts such as *under-over, top-bottom* take longer than normal to master. This leads to difficulty following group instructions.

- **Lack of fine motor skills:** This set of skills affects handwriting, cutting, pasting, table accidents (spilling), and other similar activities. These children hold pencils awkwardly, press too hard, vary size of letters, and have many erasures and scratched-out words. They have trouble taking dictation. *How long it takes a student to copy a paragraph is significant in making a diagnosis.*

- **Auditory (sound) problems:** A student may have trouble hearing sounds and telling the difference in one sound and another. For example, *lid, led, lad,* sound the same; so do *weather* and *whether.* If there is a problem with hearing, this problem is in addition to the dyslexia. When auditory impairment is the predominant characteristic, children may be diagnosed with auditory dyslexia. The sounds are mixed up on the way to the brain or in the brain. We as teachers must speak clearly and distinctly, and students must not drop endings such as *bend/bent, snack/snatch*.

- **Poor ability to organize:** This refers to their work as well as their lives. They need structure at home and school: set procedures, definite routines, and exact times. For example, children may do their homework and then leave it at home. I tell them, "When you take something out of your book bag, always put it back as soon as you finish, and leave your book bag daily in the same place." Therefore, they are not likely to leave for school without their work or miss the bus looking for the book bag. These students are also easily overwhelmed when given several tasks or steps at the same time. On paper, they may start a list of words going across the paper, then shift to writing downward in column style. They may start in the middle of a line or crowd a word at the end of the line until the word is illegible.

- **Poor conception of time as well as a delay in learning to tell time:** If parents say, "Be home in thirty minutes," children may be gone two hours and wonder why they get in trouble for not obeying their parents.

- **Visual perception problems:** This problem may show itself through reversals such as *was/saw* or *gril* for *girl.* When I was helping Dr. Shedd screen, he had each student draw a picture of a *girl* and a *boy* and then label the pictures *girl* or *boy*. We helpers laughingly started diagnosing based on how students wrote *girl* and we did not miss a lot. They would spell *girl* as *gril*. On the other hand, reversals are normal in young children. Conservatively, if reversals persist beyond first grade, along with other indications, I would become concerned.

- **Weak visual memory:** Our students cannot remember a word from the way it looks. Therefore, they do poorly with the whole-language or look-say method. Parents often say, "My child can get the big word but not the little word." Typically, there is more to look different about longer words than words of two or three letters. This is not a problem with the eyes but rather a problem in the central nervous system. Feeling the word on a rough surface brings all the sensory modalities into use at the same time. As the student writes on a rough surface with the index finger of the dominant hand (tactile, kinesthetic), looks at his finger (sight), says the word aloud, spells aloud, and then says the word again (auditory), the message is received in the brain through multiple senses. Thus, the student is using the auditory, visual and tactile senses plus the large muscles. Cursive writing, not printing, helps. When letters are joined together, reversals in writing are practically eliminated.

Caution: I often hear the public (educators and parents alike) say a person is or is not dyslexic because that person does or does not reverse letters and numbers. This is a misconception. Dyslexia is not synonymous with reversals. In fact, a person can be dyslexic without showing a pattern of reversals. Likewise, we who are not dyslexic may reverse occasionally. While working on this book, friends, trying to be helpful, suggested that I title the book *When Backward is Forward*. No way, for I would be reinforcing a misconception. Some characteristics are only detected by highly sophisticated tests. I am prone to call dyslexia "the invisible disability." True, we cannot see dyslexia as we see the autistic child, the orthopedically impaired, or the partially sighted. Researchers in laboratories, using fMRIs, can see the difference between the dyslexic and the normal brain.

- **Slowness in finishing work:** Students, fearing they will be the last one in class to finish, may rush through their work and finish on time but with many mistakes. After all, who wants to hear repeatedly from a classmate or teacher, "Aren't you done yet? Hurry up slowpoke. Get going, pokey?" Too often students will bring home classwork to finish in addition to homework. Parents of elementary students tell me that they spend as much as three hours nightly helping their children with homework. Parents and children both end up frustrated and in tears.

For the students to miss recess at school and end up spending that much time on homework is torturous. I do not intend to chastise teachers for keeping students in at recess to finish work. I have done this. Most teachers are frustrated and desperately need assistance from multisensory certified personnel. What about the single parent who works evenings? What about the parent who does not realize the importance of homework support?

While teaching first grade, I have phoned parents of students who were misbehaving and not doing their work in class to hear a parent (usually the mother) say, "I can't do anything with him at home either." How sad, dyslexic or non-dyslexic, to be out of control at this age.

Copying from the board is especially slow. The student finally finds his place on the board looks at his paper on his desk, finds his place, then forgets how to spell a word, has to look back at the board, and then repeats the process.

- **Variability in performance**: Students may do well one day and very poorly the next day on the very same material. They may know a word in one paragraph and not the next. In an effort to stabilize the variability in performance, mastery teaching and rote learning must be used. An example of mastery learning: When I am driving my car and come upon a red light, I do not process this consciously. "Red light. Stop. Put foot on break. Push down." If I went through this process, I would run the red light. I just respond appropriately; that is mastery learning.

Dyslexics have trouble generalizing. For example, we cannot teach sounds or rules in isolation. We must help the student use that sound in decoding a word and not wait for him to make that transfer step.

- **Impaired concentration ability**: Often students have a short attention span for their age. They may be hyperactive or hypoactive. Attention Deficit Hyperactive Disorder (ADHD) can take different forms and types. In one type, persons have trouble sitting, are impulsive, do not "look before they leap." They are physically active, whereas students with Attention Deficit Disorder (ADD) have an inability to concentrate. The mind is overly active but not the body. Persons affected with ADD are harder to spot. Hypoactive children are sleepy and sluggish. They feel much like someone who has just eaten a huge Thanksgiving meal. When I worked at the Reading Institute at Berea, Dr. Shedd had a platform table the correct height for standing and writing in my room. When students found it difficult to sit or got sleepy and sluggish, they felt free to leave their seats, stand, and continue their work at the writing platform.

- **Reading disabilities:** A very bright student can be reading on grade level and yet have a reading disability in terms of potential. On the other hand, a student taught through a multisensory program may have been remediated to the point of performing well in reading.

    Dyslexic children and children with AD/HD have some similar characteristics. The dyslexic child is prone to read very poorly orally yet comprehend surprisingly well, whereas the predominately ADHD student often can read words fluently but does not comprehend. Some diagnosticians use a discrepancy between a passage that is read aloud to the student and one the student reads silently in helping to diagnose dyslexia.

- **Writing disabilities (dysgraphia):** Dr. Shedd included dysgraphia and dyscalculia (math) with the characteristics of dyslexia. Today, many authorities consider them separate disabilities. Not all persons with dyslexia have writing or math weaknesses. Even today, I rarely get a referral with a diagnosis of dysgraphia or dyscalculia aside from dyslexia.

Writing disabilities are usually associated with fine motor problems discussed earlier. Among the manifestations are holding the pencil incorrectly, mark-overs and insertions, omissions, lots of erasures, letter size, and organizing ideas.

We may never get perfection in handwriting but we must insist that it be legible. As soon as possible, have the students begin cursive writing. First graders can learn cursive writing. Have students trace the cursive letter with the index finger of the dominant hand, saying the name of the letter, making the sound, then saying the name again.

Even though there are arrows in a book showing students the directions for the finger, we may have to take the student's finger and move it for him. Each step is then repeated three times correctly. We repeat the same procedure on a rough surface, again taking hold of the finger and seeing that the finger is moving in the right direction until he can do so independently. The student is now ready to write on special paper, which helps proportion the size of letters. Since cursive writing is not taught in the classroom until mid-second grade, this student may be ahead of his classmates for the first time in his life. What a boost to his self-confidence. Today students are not required to use cursive writing. How tragic for the dyslexic who has trouble with reversals and spacing. Is the computer the answer?

Writing disabilities also refer to students' inability to put on paper what they know so brilliantly in their minds. They can excel if given an oral test in content areas such as social studies or science.

- **Spotty performance on intelligence tests**: Performance on IQ tests is high in some areas, low in others. Generally, as students with dyslexia get older, IQ scores decline. In fact, it is sometimes difficult to get accurate IQ scores. Intelligence is not just something that one is born with. The characteristics of dyslexia may interfere with both acquiring information and test taking.

During this writing, I received a phone call from a distraught mother whose son seemed to be a victim to this process. Her son with dyslexia had been receiving services through special education. Through a routine re-evaluation by the school psychologist, the pupil scored a few points lower on his IQ test than the previous one; therefore, he did not meet the requirements to continue in special education according to the school's criteria. The school was using the discrepancy formula where there must be a certain number of points between intelligence and achievement. With his intelligence quotient lower, less should be expected of him academically. The discrepancy formula is no longer required under the Individual with Disabilities

Education Act for special education placement. States have the right to decide. However, the parent did not know this and was unable to negotiate for her child. The discrepancy formula is still in use today.

- **Mild speech and language problems:** There may be slurring, repetitions, hesitations, and incomplete sentences as well as delayed language development in general. Substituting a word of similar meaning may be noticed as well as reversals of sounds in speaking. For example, *animal* might be *aminal* or *elephant* might come out as *lephant*.

- **Impaired reproduction of tonal pattern:** Students may read in a monotone or a strained voice, which does not sound relaxed or natural. Common signs are ignoring punctuation marks and inappropriate change in pitch or loudness of voice (inflections).

- **Non-specific motor awkwardness**: Dyslexics run into objects as big as trees and are accident-prone.

- **Poor spelling ability**: The dyslexic's best grade may be in spelling because he has worked hard to memorize the words. However, two weeks later, when writing a manuscript, these words will be spelled incorrectly. The words are quickly forgotten.

- **Field-dependent perception**: The *field* refers to the overall visual area. For example, the *field* would be the forest as opposed to the individual trees. Dyslexics tend to look at everything rather than the important parts. They are overwhelmed by too much information presented at once. Similar visual messages tend to be confusing. As the student advances to longer words, which he is unable to recognize, he must break the word in syllables. He needs to cover all parts except the most common syllable. Sometimes by decoding that one syllable, he can figure out the entire word. If not, he uncovers another syllable.

- **Dyscalculia (math)**: The student may do well as long as he does not have to read the problem, or he may exhibit reversals in numbers as in letters. If the student has dyscalculia, he is often dyslexic also. As we become more adept at diagnosing dyscalculia, we may find more stand-alone cases. If the diagnosis is confirmed, the student should get appropriate teaching as soon as possible. Research has shown repeatedly, that the earlier the child is started on an appropriate program of remediation, the faster and easier the problem is corrected. The brain is more malleable in young children. Thus, retraining is easier. The self-concept is undamaged by failure and the child has less "catching up" to do. Young children correctly taught may never have significant lasting effects.

In summary, I do reading evaluations. I leave the diagnosing of dyslexia to psychologists—some psychologists. When I began my work, I thought I had to be professional and not tell parents that they should go to one particular diagnostician. I was wrong. Today, I only refer parents to a psychologist whose work is familiar to me. Generally, school psychologists evaluate for placement. Psychologists in private practice are more likely to make a diagnosis.

Chapter 4
ADHD and Dyslexia

I am a part of all I have met.

—Alfred Lord Tennyson

ADHD and dyslexia may coexist. Therefore, I feel the issue deserves more in-depth coverage. In a Fact Sheet provided by the International Dyslexia Association, ADHD and dyslexia are distinct conditions that frequently overlap. IDA's information also says, "ADHD is one of the most common developmental problems, affecting three to five percent of the school population …. It is estimated that thirty percent of those with dyslexia also have ADHD."[9]

According to Nancy Mather, Ph. D., University of Arizona, "With ADHD there are more behavioral kinds of problems."[10] Dyslexia is limited to reading, writing, and speaking. The student begins to wiggle, finds excuses to break from his work, and tunes out. Dr. Mather says similar areas of the brain are involved in both disorders. She goes on to say: "Both appear to lead to problems with executive function,[11] memory, and processing symbols quickly. Children with these disorders often have normal to high intelligence and high creativity, but are frustrated academically."

ADHD was identified in 1902. *The Diagnostic and Statistical Manual*, 4th edition, [12] lists three subtypes:

1. ADHD - *Predominantly Inattentive* - This type is characterized by distractibility and difficulty sustaining mental effort and attention.

2. *Predominately Hyperactive-impulsive* - This type is characterized by fidgeting with hands and feet, squirming in one's chair, acting as if driven by a motor, interrupting and intruding upon others.

3. *ADHD-Combined* – This type meets both sets of inattention and hyperactive-impulsive criteria.

A parent may have to be patient and work with the physician to get the right medication and the correct dosage. Sometimes parents will object to medication for their child, which is their right.

When a physician prescribes medication and the parents appear to hesitate, I recommend that they try medication and see if it works. As a teacher, I have seen medication make a drastic, positive change in a student. As soon as the student walked in my door, I could tell if he had taken his medicine.

On the other hand, I have also observed no difference when a physician placed an ADHD student on medication. In my experience, a student is much more likely to be diagnosed if he has ADHD with overt hyperactivity—characteristics which can be seen. With inattentive individuals who daydream and cannot stay focused, the characteristics are more subtle. Parents and teachers may not see that physical manifestation. ADD students may try so hard to concentrate that they tire more easily, which leads to activity.

Some parents have the fear that medication for ADHD will contribute to drug addiction later in life. The reverse is true. Maia Szalavitz, author and neuroscience journalist for *Times*.com, summarizes some of the research data. "If the individual is correctly diagnosed with ADHD, medicating with stimulants like Ritalin may reduce the risk of drug addiction."[13] She goes on to say: "One review of the research found a ninety-percent reduction in addiction cases for those who were given medication for ADHD compared to those who were not." However, she cautions parents to keep stimulant medications away from those who want to misuse drugs.

I once had a first-grade student who, without my recommendation or knowledge, was taken for a psychological evaluation. With the psychological evaluation in hand, the mother took her daughter to her pediatrician, and he prescribed stimulant medication. Upon questioning the child, I learned she was not taking the medication. With further checking, the mother appeared to be reselling the stimulant. I reported the situation to the prescribing physician.

This year I received a phone call from an older father. Under court order, his seventeen-year-old son was attending an alternative school. A teacher had mentioned that his son might be dyslexic. As a result, the father had the son screened. Yes, he was dyslexic and reading on fourth-grade level.

The father said, "What do I do now? The alternative school has no one trained to teach a person with dyslexia." Unfortunately, I had to tell him that the prognosis was not good for someone that age and so far behind in reading.

He went on to say, "When Jeremy was in the primary grades, he was tested for ADHD. He has been on medication for years for this problem."

Apparently, the psychologist had diagnosed the ADHD, which led to his physician's prescribing medication. However, no one had even suspected dyslexia at the time, and his dyslexia went undetected for years. What might he do now? He can certainly attend our weekly tutorial program for persons with dyslexia. However, has he given up on himself? If so, will he attend regularly and stay with the program long enough to make progress?

Physicians usually treat ADHD, which is a medical problem. Psychologists usually diagnose dyslexia, and it is an educational problem. Education is the prescription.

As a private tutor, I find some students especially challenging after a long day at school. Their ADHD medication is wearing off. Sometimes parents do not want students to have additional medication close to the tutoring appointment. The parents believe medication will interfere with appetite or sleeping. I have had to say to parents, "Your child is not going to make the progress that he would make if he were medicated." The parents have the right to make the final decision.

At the Reading Research Institute at Berea, Dr. Shedd's approach was to deal with ADHD symptoms with diet. Sandy Newmark, M. D., quoted in the winter 2011 issue of *ADDitude* magazine said this: "I have used nutritional interventions for hundreds of children with ADHD during the past twenty-four years. In many cases, dietary changes have improved the symptoms of hyperactivity, concentration, and impulsivity..." [14]

The key seems to be in stopping blood-sugar spikes. According to Dr. Newmark, the single most important thing is to reduce the amount of sugar in the ADHD student's diet. Processed carbohydrates quickly change into glucose, so the effect is almost the same as eating sugar from a spoon. She recommends eating foods rich in protein while avoiding processed sugars.

There is no one food that is a trigger for all children. Generally, parents and physicians will determine the most likely culprits and remove those foods from the child's diet one at a time. After the appropriate time for that food to get out of a child's system, they introduce another suspected food, observe behavior, and watch for unwelcome changes. This procedure is called the elimination diet.

I have read no research to prove cause and effect of diet on behavior that would stand up in academia. I often talk with parents about diet. From my observations, many parents appear to have pinpointed triggers for their child. In addition to sugar and refined carbohydrates, parents have found red dye to be a significant problem. Occasionally I find a young child, when offered candy or Kool-Aid, say, "I can't have that; it makes me hyper." I commend these parents for their insight and child rearing practices.

Personally, I think the relationship between certain foods and hyperactivity exists. However, the proof is still empirical. As my research project for my second master's degree, I wanted to investigate the effect of refined carbohydrates on reading test scores.

My college advisor thought it a terrific project, and I was excited. However, as we planned the specifics, we realized there were too many variables to control.

Chapter 5

Rubber Meets the Road

"Opportunity is missed by most people because it is dressed in overalls and looks like work."

—Thomas Edison

The second day of training Dr. Shedd bopped into the classroom looking as revived as a wilted rose newly watered. He started talking as he seated himself on the front of the teacher's desk, leaving his short legs dangling. Often he would hop down, race to the dusty chalkboard and start scribbling. He spoke quickly, with little pause between words, reminding me of a juggler deftly handling three balls in the air at the same time. He wore faded jeans, and the tail of his plaid shirt hung loosely around his hips—he smelled of tobacco.

Dr. Shedd spent the day teaching us how to apply the principles taught the day before. This was another ten-hour, exhausting day. I received my assignment. I was to teach three one-hour classes of auditory discrimination in the morning and the same three classes for another hour each in the afternoon. I had one free hour in the morning and another in the afternoon for scoring papers and recording work. I was to teach groups of ten to fifteen students. Other beginning tutors worked with one student at a time—four hours of tutoring each morning and afternoon. They worked with four students a day.

Feeling anxious about my duties, I mustered the courage to ask Dr. Shedd, "Why have I been given the task of working with twelve to fifteen students at a time when other tutors are working one-to-one?"

He stared at me and then answered bluntly, "You are a teacher. You can handle this. Mr. Marsh will demonstrate for you tomorrow. You will teach the class, and Mr. Marsh will then critique you." Fear tingled up my spine as I walked away determined to handle whatever was thrown at me. I had to succeed. Dyslexics were depending on me.

The following day, my first class arrived quietly and orderly. Students had come mainly from the southeastern part of the United States. The students were grouped by age. This class was primarily boys— some not much younger than I.

A few had been in juvenile detention centers. One had poured kerosene on herself and had just ignited the kerosene when her mother discovered her. After she spent a brief time in a psychiatric hospital, her parents, out of desperation, sent her to the Reading Institute.

Their grim, stoic faces spoke of hopelessness—the left out children with the invisible disability.

Mr. Marsh arrived. "Are you ready to get started?" he asked.

"I am." That was only a half-truth. My hands trembled, my heart raced out of control, and the rest of my body felt numb.

"Repeat these words after me," he said to the students. He said the words loudly and clearly, with only a slight pause between them. With all students standing, they repeated "*apple, after, and, apt.*" Mr. Marsh had them sit. "Now raise your right hand if you hear the same vowel in each word." Loudly and clearly, he went "*tam-ten, ram-rum, cab-tab, rat-bat, tin-tan, ban-bin.*" Student hands went up and down. A few students raised the left hand instead of the right and seemed unconscious of a mistake. Then he had students write their name on a sheet of paper.

"This time I am going to say two words, and I want you to write both vowels you hear," he told the class and had the class repeat the instructions back to him.

How did the students have time to think the sounds, much less write them? After watching for about thirty minutes, Mr. Marsh handed me the auditory book and watched me briefly. I had managed to focus so intently on Mr. Marsh that some of my anxiety had subsided. He disappeared before the end of my first class. I was on my own.

The purpose of the auditory-discrimination class was to help the students hear the sounds and tell the difference between one sound and another. Auditory class also increased attention span, memory, and speed of response. Oral exercises required students to speak answers clearly and distinctly in union.

Both oral and written exercises had to be paced so rapidly that other thoughts could not steal the students' attention. I had to enunciate distinctly and clearly with my volume turned to high. There could not be gaps or pauses in my presentation as I focused my entire being on holding the attention of my class.

By noontime of my second day of auditory, I was mentally and physically exhausted. I just felt I could not go on. I went to Dr. Shedd nearly in tears and pleaded with him. "Dr. Shedd, I can't do auditory. Please, please, just let me tutor like your other workers."

He looked at me without a hint of compassion and boomed out, "You can do it." I did not wait for solace or an offer of help. In defeat, I turned away for I could not let him hear the crack in my voice and see the dam break with a flood of tears. Battle lost, I was determined to succeed or die trying.

All summer, we were constantly flooded with visitors. In my teaching in the public-school system, I normally became a bit tense when visitors were observing. However, at Berea, I became so accustomed to visitors that I was oblivious to them.

Laughingly, groups remarked that I taught auditory with my entire body; that I not only used mind and voice, but my entire body swayed with the rhythm of my voice. I used such force to maintain the right volume, enunciation, and speed that my body became part of the action. No wonder my energy was depleted at the end of each day.

While the summer of 1970 was the most physically and mentally exhausting nine weeks of my life, I persevered. The long, taxing workdays were not the only stressor.

I recall late one evening walking alone across the nearly deserted campus. One of my older auditory students was walking several feet behind me. Surging in my head was the thought that he could throw a rock and hit me in the back. I was without protection, an open target for all his pent-up venom from his abuse as a nonreader. I quickened my steps as perspiration began to moisten my pores and my heart galloped like a race horse in the Kentucky Derby.

Soon after returning home, I developed respiratory problems. As a result, I took ten allergy shots per week for a year and a lesser number for ten years. While one cannot prove the cause and effect, an allergy specialist in Nashville warned me that I was destined for emphysema if I did not lower my stress and workload. Stress and determination have a price— but the elimination of injustice and oppression has rewards.

Chapter 6
Sundays at Berea

Real joy comes not from ease or riches or from the praise of men, but from doing something worthwhile.

—Sir Wilfred Grenfell

He worked every weekday from 7:30 in the morning to 5:00 at night and every other Saturday. On the long weekends, Frances and I would explore the beautiful countryside in a part of Kentucky unknown to me.

Berea is located at the foothills of the Appalachian Mountains but we were warned not to go into the mountains because mountaineers do not like strangers. After attending church in the mornings, our Sunday-afternoon drives took us through tiny towns with names like Bighill, Clover Bottom, High Bridge, and Bernice. We passed old cemeteries, heard the soothing water from waterfalls, and saw the glistening, clear blue water of slowly rolling streams.

Wildflowers grew everywhere—goldenrod, Queen Anne's lace, and black-eyed Susan. Occasionally, we would see a blue jay or a hummingbird. A usual sight was a coal-black crow with its wings outstretched, as it left its dead prey with a strident caw. Occasionally, we spotted wild blackberries along a country road. Once we stopped along the road and enjoyed the succulent treat beside a steep hill. As we passed a persimmon tree, I longed to put a ripe orange persimmon in my mouth and feel that mellow wild fruit against my palate.

As Berea was a world-renowned art-and-craft center, either alone or with Frances, I would browse the shops and marvel at what talent, persistence, and patience could produce from an ordinary block of wood. I saw beautiful busts, vases, and bowls and even dulcimers. There was also dyeing and weaving, pottery, and ironworks. It helped us escape from the weekday stress.

Kentucky is famous for its state parks. One such nearby park was Boonesborough State Park, named after Daniel Boone, who first explored the area. One of our Sunday-afternoon excursions was to this cool, carefree site. We relaxed on a bench under massive trees, each trying to tiptoe above the other to grab its share of the sun. It was at this spot, near rustic cabins and the tranquil Kentucky River, that I told Frances the story of Don.

Don Before Berea

Don's principal referred him to me in September 1969. He was nine years old and in a class for the mentally retarded, a term used at that time for students far below average in intelligence. However, the same referral form showed he had obtained a Stanford-Benet IQ [15] of 102, well within the average range. On the Peabody Picture Vocabulary Test, he had an IQ of 107. I administered the Slosson Intelligence Test [16] where he earned an IQ of 93. [17]

"I have never been able to understand why Don was in a class for mentally retarded children," I remarked to Frances.

Frances spoke up. "I bet the school system didn't know what else to do with him! That happens in my school district."

"Frances, you are so right. Even his special-education teacher didn't want to keep this bright boy in her class. But I can see Don now walking into my tiny work area in an add-on building at our junior high school," I said sadly.

This building had four classrooms. Our classroom was divided into thirds. The first area was the reception area with a clerical assistant. My work area was the middle area, and a second teacher occupied the back area. The partitions and walls were brightly painted in shades of pink and blue—probably from leftover paint.

The three-area classroom still smelled of fresh paint that mingled with an air of cleanliness. Don was quiet and expressionless. As he took off his coat and placed it in the reception area, I could see scars on his left arm.

"Don, how is school going for you this year?" I asked.

He shrugged his shoulders and let out a long sigh. He mumbled, "Not too good."

"Can you tell me more about what you mean?"

In a louder voice that left no doubt about his feelings, he said, "I hate school."

"Why do you hate school?"

"I am with the dummies all day. They pick fights with me even when I try to be nice to them. Then the teacher makes me stay in for recess." Don's voice trailed off but he was beginning to relate to me. I let him go on spilling his school frustrations.

Finally, I shifted to home. "Don, what do you do at home for fun?"

Don talked about the typical likes of seventh-grade boys: basketball with friends, TV, movies, hikes in the nearby woods.

"Tell you what I don't like at home." Now Don was beginning to take over the conversation.

"Go ahead. I'm listening."

"I can't read. When I was younger, my dad would sit me down beside him and tell me I was going to read or else, and it was usually else." Don's voice was getting louder and louder. I could almost see the flames of anger blaze upward from his fiery eyes.

"Dad told me I was dumb. I must be. Why else can I not read? As I grew older, Dad would ground me for weeks when I brought my report card home."

What my minister had said in a sermon shortly before I left home rang true: "Broken bones heal much faster than words spoken inappropriately."

I knew Sundays were a time of relaxation and rest, but I just had to share this burden with Francis. She was one of the few persons who truly understood.

Don had received counseling at the local mental-health center. Prior to that, he had been evaluated at a hospital connected with Fort Bragg, a military base in North Carolina. He knew sixteen of one-hundred twelve of the Dolch Basic Sight Words: *all, had, help, brown, cold, I, at, is, hot, can, a, little, five, and, green, look.*

Don did not read well enough to score on the Gilmore Oral Reading Test [18] for grades one through eight and missed all but two words on The St. Louis Public Schools Diagnostic Spelling Test. He spelled *man* and *one*. Essentially, Don was a non-reader.

On Don's referral form, the referring teacher wrote: "In four years, Don had a broken collarbone, a broken leg, and caught his left arm in a conveyer belt." That was why I saw the scar on his arm when I first met him.

As I was telling Frances about these accidents, she interrupted. "Look at the horrendous number of accidents that our reading institute students are having. Don't you remember Dr. Shedd's telling us that many of these children are accident prone?"

"Oh, yes, I had not made the connection. Dr. Shedd described many of these children as being impulsive—they act before they think. Since they are inattentive, they just don't pay attention to that sharp blade or the car coming down the road."

When I returned home, I managed to get Don evaluated by Dr. Shedd. Dr. Shedd felt he was both dyslexic and ADHD (attention deficit hyperactive disorder). The latter most likely accounted for all the accidents he had.

Don After Berea

Using my multisensory training, I worked with Don at the reading clinic two hours a week until the federal funds ran out and I was assigned elsewhere. He missed 133 Dolch Sight Words in the beginning, now he knew almost all 220 of them. He went from a non-reader to a score of 3.0 (third grade) on vocabulary and 2.7 (second grade, seventh month) on comprehension as measured by the Gilmore Oral Reading Test.

Considering the little time spent with him and his "I can't" attitude, he made excellent progress but was far from being a proficient reader. Today, we are hearing with increasing frequency, from researchers such as Dr. Gordon Sherman,[19] Dr. Kenneth Pugh,[20] Dr. Maryanne Wolf,[21] and others concerning the plasticity of a young child's brain. Older children and adults do not have the same brain plasticity to generate new nerve cells and retrain the brain. Now, I better understand what may have accounted for our slow progress.

As the sun headed toward the western horizon, Frances interrupted with, "You need to shush and we need to head back toward campus. Two ladies do not need to meet up with darkness in this wilderness." In addition to the imminent darkness, I think Frances felt I was telling her nothing new. I think there were Dons in her part of the South also.

Dyslexia and Abstractions

Feeling a need to repent of the gloomy overcast I had created by talking about Don's plight, I forced myself into a more jovial mood. "Frances, I gave an assignment to a group of excellent seventh-grade readers during my second year of teaching in the public-school system. The task was to read a book and decorate the cover. Instead of saying *book cover*, I said, *book jacket*."

I looked over at Frances. Her eyes began to laugh. Either Frances knew students with dyslexia or she was reading my mind.

"Yes, this student, who was rarely faithful in doing his homework, brought in a treasure. It was a beautiful brown army jacket with appliqué of scenes from the book he had read. The stitches were neatly done. The variety of colors added sparkle to the drab jacket. Oh, I think he had even splattered glitter in places."

"What did you do?" Frances was quick to ask.

"My mouth flew open ready to say, 'You misunderstood the assignment. That was not what I told you to do. Don't you ever listen?' Fortunately, I enthusiastically said, 'Oh, what a brilliant idea—a real jacket. You have really put a lot of work into this.' Of course, his mother could have done the sewing for him; but I knew he deserved praise without an interrogation."

Frances popped up and said, "You know dyslexics take words concretely, literally, or they may have trouble retrieving the correct word. At our house, we have 'leftovers' after a big meal. After Thanksgiving one year, I had a student return to school telling me he had 'scrapovers' at his house. Have you looked at the book Dr. Shedd talked about in our staff meeting?"

"Oh, you are referring to idioms like, 'A stitch in time saves nine'," I answered.

"Yes, abstractions. We need to talk to them in literal terms. Instead of your idiom, we should say something like, 'If we can keep a problem from occurring, we can avoid a lot more trouble later'," Frances explained.

A Laughing Matter

As I drove my white Mustang through the narrow back roads to campus, I told Frances one more incident that happened the previous week; my pencils kept disappearing. Since there were five minutes between classes, I had my students leave their pencils on their desks for the next class. It seemed so pointless to take pencils from students as they passed through the door and then reissue them as new students entered five minutes later. Each student needed at least two pencils because they could not stop to sharpen a pencil. A few cons tried to break the lead on purpose.

I was forever saying, "Leave your pencils on your desks. I do not see your pencil. Come back. You forgot to leave your pencil."

As a new class entered, students kept reporting, "I don't have a pencil." This always happened after I had gotten everyone's attention and was ready to dive into an auditory drill with breakneck speed. It got to be irritating. I was going into the staff office every other morning asking for another box of pencils.

Mr. Marsh, Sister Marie, or whoever was staffing the office would say, "Oh no, not you again, Miss Fuller (my maiden name). What are your students doing with those pencils?"

I was embarrassed but tried to make a joke out of the situation by saying, "How many came to 'sick call' for tummy aches today?"

Finally, the mystery of the disappearing pencils was resolved. One morning before class, I heard Mr. Marsh bellow, "Miss Fuller, come into my office!"

I despairingly jumped to my feet, knocking papers to the floor. *What now?* I wondered as I rushed into the main office and found Mr. Marsh, smiling behind a stack of books.

"I found out last night what's been going on with all your pencils. The boys had a contest to see who could collect the most pencils. We found 467 hoarded in the boys' dorm last night. Thomas and Paul were infuriated over losing the swimming match, so they 'ratted' and led us to the pile of pencils."

I was so gullible to their scheme. Falling victim to the conning nature of some students with dyslexia was another lesson learned. Frances and I laughed together.

Then she said, "Do you really think there were four-hundred-sixty-seven pencils in the boys' dorm?"

"Yes, I understand Mr. Marsh supervised the boys as they counted the pencils." Laughing repeatedly restored our sanity. Shortly, we were back on campus.

Chapter 7

Our Final Evening at Berea

Do every act as if it were your last.

— Marcus Aurelius

Hooray. The nine weeks were over. One of the most revered times was the last evening—a time of debriefing and bringing closure. Many of us sat on the same bare floor that smelled a little like the oiled floor in the one-room school I attended as a child.

That first evening seemed so long ago. Dr. Shedd sat next to his assistant, Mr. Collins. Dr. Shedd was a workaholic. He worked seven days a week and would sleep while his driver took him from one state to another. Often he would not take time to sit for a nutritious meal. He replenished his energy by keeping a can of peanuts close by. A cigarette was usually in his hand or in an ashtray nearby.

As the summer progressed, it seemed Dr. Shedd spoke with more urgency and did more, faster. Tonight his lack of sleep showed up in dark-purple blotches under his eyes. His chin had an uncharacteristic sag.

I had not thought of him as a deeply religious person even though he would sometimes refer to God in his daily staff meetings.

Dr. Shedd had been speaking to my head but that evening he wrote on my heart. All was somber except for the swish of wind blowing the soft white curtains through the open window and the occasional chirp of a cricket. Dr. Shedd began his farewell message by reading from Ecclesiastes, 3: 1-8:

> *To everything there is a season, and a time to every purpose under the heaven:*
>
> *A time to be born, and a time to die; a time to plant, and a time to pluck up that which is planted;*
>
> *A time to kill, and a time to heal; a time to break down, and a time to buildup;*
>
> *A time to weep, and a time to laugh; a time to mourn, and a time to dance;*
>
> *A time to cast away stones, and a time to gather stones together; a time to embrace, and a time to refrain from embracing;*
>
> *A time to get, and a time to lose; a time to keep, and a time to cast away;*
>
> *A time to rend, and a time to sew; a time to keep silence, and a time to speak;*
>
> *A time to love, and a time to hate; a time of war, and a time of peace....*

The Bible KJV

Little did we know that in four years this man, small and frail in his physique but a giant in zeal to help persons with dyslexia, would be dead at age fifty-four.

PART TWO

HOME

Chapter 8
Gearing Up

Apply yourself. Get all the education you can, but then, by God, do something. Don't just stand there, make it happen.

—Lee Iacocca

My compassionate and supportive friends from home cheered me with their letters while I was away. They made statements such as "the students are fortunate to have such a kind, gentle teacher as you." Being a shy, benign person, I wrote back, "I am taking lessons on being mean." By that I meant I had to be strict, stern, and tough. These attributes did not flow naturally. We had to be vigilant and assertive so no hole in our structure could be breached. Yet the pencil incident made me understand that I needed more practice.

While I was away at Berea, parents and community volunteers at home had not been idle. They filed articles of incorporation to establish an organization called The Christian County Association for Specific-Perceptual Motor Disability. We were to be an affiliate of a state organization bearing that name. [22] Soon after, we became an independent organization, and according to my research, we have outlived our parent organization.

In doing research for this book, I found a 2011 article that referred to Dr. Shedd's work in Baton Rouge, Louisiana. The article[23] stated: "From his research, Shedd created a program for the prison system of Kentucky to teach inmates how to read." The article says that at one time more than two-hundred institutions had similar programs based on Shedd's work.

It goes on to say "Shedd came to Baton Rouge in the early 1970s to conduct seminars. This led to a Saturday tutorial program, then to a summer program and finally, within two years, to a school, the Charles Shedd School."

Many years later, we embraced a regional concept and incorporated as Dyslexia Association of the Pennyrile. A board of directors was established and officers selected. The plan was for me to learn how to teach students with dyslexia and to come home to supervise a community program.

Bob Stites was the "spark plug" behind our community's initiative. However, Mrs. Martha Martin, who had recently moved to Hopkinsville from

Louisville, Kentucky, planted the idea. Mrs. Martin's dyslexic son had experienced heartbreaking struggles in learning to read until his parents enrolled him in a community program in Louisville. When Mrs. Martin came to Hopkinsville, she found no help. Frantic to get her son back on track, she shared her anguish at a PTA meeting at St. Peter and Paul School.

> *My son, Chris, had failed third grade. We were spending two hours every night on reading and other homework. I would end up in utter frustration. I would yell at him and then feel guilty because I knew he was trying in earnest.*
>
> *Every time I went for a conference, his teacher said he was inattentive, lazy, and immature. Finally, in third grade, the school tested him. He was reading on the first-grade level. He scored poorly on phonetics, decoding, vocabulary, and comprehension. Of course, if he could not recognize the words, his vocabulary and comprehension would be low. Nothing the school did or I did seemed to help.*

The group sat in silence. After a long pause, she told them of a low-cost community program in Louisville that had changed her son's life—in fact, the entire family.

As Bob and Theresa Stites listened to Mrs. Martin's story, it was as if she was describing their son,

Jason. The Stites had searched for eight years to find out why Jason couldn't learn to read, even though he had been evaluated by five different specialists. Each one said he was bright but gave different reasons for his problems in the classroom, yet none had mentioned dyslexia.

Mr. and Mrs. Stites began to have hope.

Mrs. Martin's passionate pleas persuaded the PTA to finance Dr. Charles Shedd, consultant to the program in Louisville, to come to Hopkinsville to speak in late 1969.

Start-up Funds

Even though the organization was established when I returned home, we had no start-up money. Starting our campaign for funds, President Bob Stites made an appointment for both of us to see a philanthropic acquaintance, Frank Yost. Mr. Bob picked me up at my apartment and we drove to an affluent neighborhood.

After we rang the doorbell, Mr. Yost ushered us into his library, the likes of which I had never seen. The four walls were lined with books from floor to ceiling. As our feet sank into the plush white carpet, Mr. Yost invited us to sit at an antique walnut table. Mr. Bob explained the purpose of our visit. I interrupted occasionally to explain about dyslexia and the necessity for these children to be taught in a way they can learn.

To our utter amazement, our host quickly said, "I will donate five-hundred dollars." In 1970, five-hundred dollars was a lot of money. A few years later, the association became an agency of United Way, which solved a lot of the fundraising burden until the economic crunch started in 2009.

As we left, Mr. Bob said, "Did I hear right? Did he really say he would donate five-hundred dollars?"

"Yes, Mr. Bob," I replied jubilantly. That was the end of our fundraising—we had enough money to invite Dr. Shedd back for a workshop to train our parent tutors and buy books and supplies.

Mr. and Mrs. Stites' passion, sacrifice, and untiring efforts, drew other desperate parents and sympathetic community leaders into this vision. Mr. and Mrs. Stites' mission has grown and is very much alive today, some forty-two years later. We have an office with a secretary for ten hours a week. In addition to the teaching program, we do monthly screenings and provide community education. We also helped get a dyslexia bill through the legislature.

.

Chapter 9
First Tutorial Program

I am not what happens to me. I am what I choose to become.

—Carl Jung

In the fall of 1970, we started our first tutorial program with twenty students. The youngest student was seven and the oldest sixteen. Dr. Shedd had diagnosed all children participating in the program with either dyslexia or hyperkinesis.[24]

The local school system donated housing for the program. My home was the office, and my phone doubled as the office phone. I was not only director but secretary as well. Even our stationery bore my home address. Eventually, my husband and I ran out of room in our garage for our cars because I had accumulated so much dyslexia material.

Program Procedure

For a child to enroll in the program, one parent had to work in the program or be responsible for getting someone in his/her place. All tutors received training through Dr. Shedd's workshops. For a period after Dr. Shedd's death, the tutors and I would arise at four a.m. and drive to Louisville for workshops. All tutoring was under my constant supervision. Parents never worked with their own child. There had to be a teacher/student relationship. A student was rotated from one tutor to another several times during a semester. Another purpose of the rotation was to give each student the advantage of the strengths of different tutors. Each tutor participated in staff training during the three-hour period.

Having one or both parents participate has many advantages. The student reasons, "If this program is important enough for Mom or Dad to take off work early or drive one–hundred-seventy miles round-trip, tutoring must be something very important." Thus, student motivation and confidence in the method are increased. Second, as the parent or parents learn multisensory techniques, he or she can help the child apply these to homework. Third, the parent or parents can take part in group meetings. The benefits of joining a support group include learning about dyslexia from each other, finding they are not alone in their struggles, and picking up tips on structure at home.

Method

Instruction is explicit, systematic, sequential, and multisensory. The student sees, touches, hears, speaks and feels the movement of his arm as he writes with the index finger of the dominant hand.

A student feels a new word and corrects errors in reading and writing by feeling the letters on a rough surface, such as a Masonite board. We call this piece of Masonite our memory board. Any rough surface would accomplish the same result. We want the student to perceive the memory board as a teaching and learning tool, just as paper, pencils, and books are learning tools.

Up to twenty pairs of students and tutors work aloud in one large room—the louder the better. Why? A student is trained to attend only to his tutor. Once the student can maintain focus in this environment, the student will be less inclined to hear the hallway noise or the shuffling of paper inside the classroom when he returns. The noise also forces the tutor and student to speak loudly and distinctly and not to lower the voice on word endings.

This multisensory approach helps to ensure automatic memory. Review and repetition are hallmarks of this method. How many of us can remember nursery rhymes learned at age five? Mastery learning is recall that does not require us to think or even hesitate. Progression goes from the simple to the more complex, always emphasizing drill and reinforcement.

Working one-to-one, the student proceeds as fast or as slowly as necessary for mastery. Careful pacing, structured procedures, and sequential presentation combine reading, writing, and spelling. Honest, specific praise is fundamental.

In order for this organizational pattern and method to work, tutors must be properly trained and closely supervised by a professional steeped in the method. They must also be able to work well with diverse personalities.

While a high degree of education is not a requirement, there are parents who are unable to tutor in this type of setting. If parents cannot pay for a tutor, one is paid for with donated money. Success is achieved when all the necessary elements come together: proper training, application, and adherence to structure.

Chapter 10
Origin of Method

The men who make history have no time to write it.

—Metternich

Who was the person from whom Dr. Shedd derived his method of teaching persons with dyslexia? He was Dr. Samuel T. Orton, a neuropsychiatrist, who began his research in Iowa in 1919 but spent much of his professional life in New York City. He had an insatiable interest in children who looked normal, seemed bright, but were unable to read.

He tested his theories with research, accounting for much of what we know about dyslexia today. Successful methods today used with persons with dyslexia are based on the work of Dr. Orton and his colleagues. Parents, if you want a method that will work with your dyslexic child, find a properly trained Orton-Gillingham tutor who adheres to his/her training. Dr. Orton's work is to dyslexia what Sigmund Freud's work is to psychoanalysis.

Anna Gillingham was a social worker and teacher whom Dr. Orton invited to work with him. With the aid of her co-worker Bessie Stillman, Anna Gillingham put Dr. Orton's theory and research into practice. They used Dr. Orton's methods directly with students, trained teachers, and helped establish schools for persons with dyslexia.

After Dr. Orton's death in 1948, his wife, June, was instrumental in establishing the Orton Dyslexia Society, which became The International Dyslexia Association in 1997.

For a history of Dr. Orton's work along with other pioneers in dyslexia, read *DYSLEXIA...Samuel T. Orton and His Legacy*,[25] published on the fiftieth anniversary of the International Dyslexia Association.

Marcia Henry spoke at the 2011 IDA Conference, [26] recounting some of IDA's history. I was so inspired by her presentation that I wanted to visit Dr. Orton's burial site. With a little research, I learned that Dr. Orton was buried in Greenwood Cemetery in Columbus, Ohio. With only the address of Greenwood Cemetery and a picture of the Orton tombstone, I went searching for Dr. Orton's grave on Easter Sunday, 2012. The cemetery office was closed, and the site had acres of graves with thousands of tombstones. To use an old expression, finding Dr. Orton's grave was like searching for a needle in a haystack.

Just as I was about to abandon my hunt, I spotted the tombstone. One large tombstone with "Orton" in jumbo letters announced the family burial site. I surveyed individual family markers, seventeen in all.

Dr. Orton's marker was beneath the one larger tombstone. On one side was inscribed the name of his first wife, Mary Follett Orton who died in 1926, and on the other side was the name, June Lyday Orton, who died in 1977. Even though Dr. Orton died when I was eight years old, I stood in awe as I felt his presence. He is still very much alive today through the thousands who continue his work.

In my autographed copy of Marcia K. Henry's book, she wrote, "For Ruth, Best wishes in your work. You are part of the legacy."

I continue to prize that autograph and sentiment. I recall only one other equally endearing compliment about my work with dyslexia. It came from a former minister, Rev. Carmen King. He said, "Ruth, you are as much of a missionary here as a person of the church who works in a foreign county."

Thank you, Reverend King and Doctor Henry. I hope I have, am, and will, make a difference.

Chapter 11
Dr. Shedd's Contribution

The world is a dangerous place, not because of those who do evil, but because of those who look on and do nothing.

—Albert Einstein

Doctor Shedd's contribution to the Orton/Gillingham approach was to organize a system and write materials which persons with a nominal amount of training and supervision could use. Heretofore, only highly trained educators, usually working with one student at a time, were able to use the Orton/Gillingham method. Consequently, the number of persons taught with a proven method was severely limited. There were not enough trained teachers, and only the affluent could afford one of these teachers for three hours a week for possibly years.

Dr. Shedd brought life-changing help to the *common man* as well. He wrote, researched, and continually revised instructional materials. His research continued for ten summers at the Reading Research Institute at Berea College. He also did research as a professor at the University of Alabama at Birmingham. Unfortunately, he did not make the time to publish his research and record his vast knowledge during his short life. To my knowledge, he never put his research through statistical analyses so academia would accept and apply his revolutionary work.

Dr. Shedd was dogmatic and blunt. While a pioneer in delivery of successful services to dyslexic persons, he did not associate himself with the Orton Dyslexia Society and others who taught persons with dyslexia. A number of his ideas were ahead of their time. Academia probably would not have been ready to accept them. For these reasons, Dr. Shedd has never received due recognition for his highly significant work.

His method was called Alphabetic-Phonetic-Structural-Linguistic (APSL).[27] The International Multi-sensory Structured Language Education Council (IMSLEC),[28] the accrediting arm of the International Dyslexia Association, describes nine modified methods developed by professionals who were Dr. Orton's students. Five other methods, including APSL, are listed as using the tenets of the Orton-Gillingham program, but Dr. Orton and Miss Gillingham did not directly train the authors.

Joyce Pickering, Executive Director Emerita of the Shelton School for persons with dyslexia in Dallas, Texas, has been a leader in establishing standards for teachers. Ms. Pickering once worked for Dr. Shedd in

Louisiana. She continued to research, refine, and use some of his materials in this private school setting.

Chapter 12

International Dyslexia Association

"Truly rich are those who enjoy what they have."

—Yiddish Proverb

I was ecstatic with expectation as I arrived at my first International Dyslexia Association Conference in Cincinnati, Ohio, in 1992. In fact, the conference proved to be *dyslexia heaven.*

I had been a member of IDA (then the Orton Dyslexia Society) for many years. What a thrill it was to meet people who understood dyslexia and who were excited about research, diagnosis, and appropriate teaching methods. The printed journal pages came alive as I actually met and heard pioneers like Sally Childs, Margaret Rawson, and Norman Geschwind. Such leaders took on a new meaning as they became real people to me.

In a hallway or gathering area, I would gaze at a nametag and wonder who that person might be. I would try to associate a name with a person whose picture I had seen in one of the journals. Who is that

person? Is that someone accomplished in the field of dyslexia? Have I devoured this person's writings? I compared this experience to sneaking into the dining room of our nation's Capitol. "Is that senator so and so? That looks like someone very important, but who is she?"

As I contrasted this conference with a multitude of conferences, workshops, and discussions in which I had participated, I realized this conference was strikingly different. Everyone used the word *dyslexia* as if it were a common household product. *Dyslexia*—everyone knew what everyone else was saying. Previously, I left meetings fuming inwardly and feeling powerless and inept in standing up to professionals whom I considered my superiors yet who were so uninformed and smug about dyslexia.

One all-time great whose writings I had read was Dr. Roger Saunders. In fact, Dr. Saunders, whom I got to know well as I attended subsequent conferences, had worked with Dr. Orton. At this first conference, I eagerly signed-up for Dr. Saunders' session. This psychologist, diagnostician, researcher, and educator gave a stunning presentation on handwriting. Afterwards, I waited my turn to speak to him, to actually talk to someone who had known Dr. Orton. What an honor to be in his presence.

I continued to see and talk with Dr. Saunders at future IDA conferences. The last time I saw Dr. Saunders was at the IDA Conference in Denver in 2005. He was frail, his gait slow, and his balance precarious. His mind was keen as I reintroduced myself to him.

"Is all well with dyslexia in Kentucky?" he wanted to know.

"We would be better if we could get the legislature to do its job."

He chuckled as if to say, "What else is new?" I did not prolong the conversation.

I said to a friend who accompanied me, "I wonder how many more conventions Dr. Saunders will be able to attend?" My last glimpse of him was sitting with two older ladies in the nearly deserted dining room of the Adams Mark Hotel. Soon after, the news of his death deeply saddened me.

As I continue to attend the International Dyslexia Conference, my excitement has not waned. My interest has shifted somewhat from speakers to attendees: assessing the state of dyslexia through the eyes of practitioners at the grassroots level in the U. S. and abroad. My most recent conference was in 2011 in Chicago. Our office secretary is a young, energetic person with a passion for persons with dyslexia. Because our association struggles financially, it could not pay either of our expenses. I paid my expenses, except for an IDA scholarship, and helped Amy with

her expenses. As others have helped me, I was grateful
that I could help someone else.

Chapter 13
Program Director

Getting knocked down in life is a given...Getting up and moving forward is a choice.

—Zig Ziglar

As supervisor of our program, it was my responsibility to see that the materials were used effectively. There is nothing magical about the materials. The proper use brought the desired results. For this reason, APSL materials were not sold to the public. Not only did I ensure the appropriate use of the materials, I had to develop a no nonsense attitude, speak with authority, and set high standards through my example. To have a successful program, we had rules that brought structure. One rule had to do with absences. The student could miss if he or she was ill or if there was a death in the family.

One Saturday morning I awoke to the ringing of my phone. I recognized the voice of a parent tutor as she asked, "Can my son be excused from the dyslexia program this morning?"

"Why?" I asked

"He is getting married this afternoon."

Having thought I had heard every excuse invented and a few extras, I responded, "I think a groom needs to be at his wedding, so… go. " Therefore, we eventually added "or some other unusual circumstance" to our excused list.

Charlie

In that first year, we missed one of our older students. As customary, we phoned his dad. Dad was unable to tutor, and his mother was deceased.

Dad would say, "I drove Charlie to that blue building on Central Avenue, watched him get out and head toward the building."

After the third event, we positioned someone to watch for Charlie. You guessed it. He was not coming inside the building but hiding out until time for his dad to pick him up. As often happens with older students (young ones, too), they develop evasive habits. My advice for parents is: don't make excuses for your child; do not help him rationalize.

"Oh, my child didn't trash that classroom when we were on break. Someone must have done this damage after school yesterday," a parent might say. Too often, we feel a child's behavior is a reflection of us. Our self-esteem is involved. First, we should examine ourselves with honesty and then consistently hold the child accountable for his actions. I recall one of our students involved in this type of family dynamic. In a few years, on a visit to the county jail, I saw his name on the jail roster.

Growth in Adversity

As the group leader for our parent tutors, I found taking command of a group of adults agonizing. A saying that is entrenched in my consciousness is, *Do what you fear; watch it disappear*. I forged ahead and watched my shell disappear. The parent tutors were desperate for help for their children. They were a very devoted, loyal group of people who rarely questioned my actions or decisions. However, occasionally I would have to deal with a parent who "blew a fuse."

I took on this responsibility as a volunteer. While the parents paid a small fee to participate in the program, the SPMD Board [29] had not mentioned money to me. I still had college loans to repay, but what I was doing was more important than money. I was helping to change lives.

In the early days, unenlightened non-participants accused me of trying to make money by suggesting our program. Such accusations were not only false but also hurtful. I was donating my time, taking most phone calls at home, and assisting our board. I was tired.

To be slapped with doing this for profit was tough to hear and not true. Someone once said, "The only person never criticized is the person who does nothing."

In retrospect, I realize such parents were in denial. They chose to close their minds to new information and dealt with the possibility of dyslexia consistent with how they had seen family members and close friends react. It is okay to feel irate, but acting on these feelings further destroys communication. Nor is it helpful to blame. However, at that much younger stage in my life, I had not learned to react to negativity in a positive yet assertive manner. I suppressed my feelings. *Ouch, that can hurt.*

The scripture my dad sometimes read aloud in his daily Bible reading when I was a child rang in my ears: "You shall be persecuted but not forsaken." (2 Corinthians 4:9.) Such thoughts, plus the spoken and unspoken affirmations from the parents, board members, and community leaders helped propel me forward. *There is growth in adversity.*

As the parents made sacrifices, I had to model my expectations for them. If parents were expected to be on time, I had to be there fifteen minutes early. If the students could not miss, I could not miss. I recall my husband, an only child, taking his mother alone to a Nashville hospital for very serious brain surgery. Because the workshop for a new tutorial program was held the same day, I could not go. Ironically, the same scenario repeated itself on the same day the following year.

The previous surgery was not successful, and I modeled my loyalty to the program rather than family by again attending the workshop.

On another occasion, my future husband was visiting me at my apartment one evening. He was an unusually patient, kind, and understanding man. I received so many long, dyslexia-related phone calls that he arose and mumbled as he left, "If you are going to spend all evening with dyslexia, I'm leaving." He did. He called a few days later, but I had learned his benevolence had its limits.

Our program has been and is an opportunity for parents to involve themselves in order to receive help. My greatest disappointment has been parents who could engage themselves in the program but refused to make the needed sacrifices, and their child suffered.

Chapter 14

We Made a Difference

The purpose of life is to count, to matter, to make a difference that we lived at all.

— Leo Buscaglia

It was the last session of our first tutorial program. I was to retest each student with the same standardized reading test used at the beginning of the program and compare the beginning test scores with the ending. I left my stopwatch home and had to borrow someone's watch with a second hand.

Mrs. Louise Hill, who followed Bob Stites as association president, usually checked on us each Saturday morning. That day, as she quietly approached she startled me and I jumped. As I scurried down the hallway, one foot tripped over the other causing me to tumble. Humiliated, I got up unhurt.

Mrs. Hill looked baffled and asked, "Why are you so 'up-tight' today? Since this is the last day of our program, I thought you would be bouncing with delight."

I forced a smile, tried harder to suppress my feelings, and ignored her. Actually, I was apprehensive that our students would not show the gains the Louisville and Berea programs did. "Oh, ye of little faith."

Our average per-student gain was slightly more than one year after only sixteen Saturday mornings. I could not control myself. I gleefully went to Mrs. Hill and our parents with the terrific news.

Had students made that kind of progress in the regular classroom, they would have been on grade level without need for this program. However, a word of caution: just because a student is reading on grade level does not mean the student is not dyslexic and in need of help. If a dyslexic student is very bright, the student is intellectually capable of more than just reading commensurate with his grade placement.

We once had a primary student in our program with an IQ of 142, one of the highest intelligence scores I have encountered. She participated in our program only a short time because her parents and teacher felt reading was not a problem. Yes, she was doing well for her grade placement but how much better could she have done? With this IQ, the student was gifted and capable of reading far above her grade placement.

After the first program, even more important than any test scores, parents reported that students who had shown no interest in picking up a book and reading were now doing so. In addition, students were spending less time on homework.

One parent said, "Josh didn't want to be called on in the classroom. Now he doesn't mind being called on at all. He even volunteers to read. Prior to the program, he would sit in the classroom and ignore his work because he couldn't do it. The work was just too hard." Obviously, some layers of the destructive "I can't" attitude had finally been chipped away.

Chapter 15

The Unexpected

I can live for two months on a good compliment.

—Mark Twain

One of the greatest surprises of my life came after the completion of our first program. Announcements went out concerning our regular board meeting. As usual, I helped prepare the agenda. Our meeting was to take place downtown in the community room of an office building. Nothing seemed unusual except parents who had participated in the tutorial program were there as well as the board members.

Mrs. Brooks stood and said, "I move that we adjourn the business meeting."

I looked at my watch. *Was I late?*

While these thoughts raced through my head, I thought I heard Mrs. Stites say, "I second the motion."

Had I missed the business meeting?

When I realized that the board was actually skipping the business, I shouted, "Oh, no, wait. Where is the agenda?" My voice grew louder and louder as I yelled over an uproar, "We must discuss summer school and fundraising. We have to find ways to put money back in our treasury."

Over my vehement protests, the business meeting adjourned before it even started. I sat down defeated. Mrs. Hill, president, uncovered a table of elaborately wrapped packages. Everyone looked at me and yelled, "Surprise!" Those dear parents, many of them with limited finances, were giving me a surprise shower as a way of saying "thank you." No one had ever given me a birthday party like this. I joyfully opened each gift, which included a purse, a scarf, earrings, and a necklace—all very practical gifts for a young teacher. Forty-two years later, I still have some of these gifts.

As board members began bringing out refreshments, Mrs. Hill handed me an envelope with orders to open it. Tucked inside a card were five crisp new one-hundred dollar bills. I had not seen that much money at one time in my entire life. I thought I was working to make a difference. Yet I was profusely rewarded materially as well as spiritually. I was beginning to find my life. "He that loseth his life for my sake shall find it." (Matthew 10:39.)

By forgetting myself and helping others, I was beginning to glean confidence, assertiveness, and fulfillment. I changed. I started making speeches and doing workshops, and I now have no hesitancy in starting a conversation with the most esteemed person. I even pleaded unsuccessfully with one Governor, before a group of elected local officials, for funds to help dyslexic persons.

When former president Bill Clinton came to Hopkinsville campaigning for Hillary in 2009, I stood in line for hours to shake hands with him. He had mentioned in his speech another area of exceptionality. I was in a huff because I thought dyslexia should have had "equal time."

When President Clinton reached me, I said, "Mr. Clinton, don't forget about persons with dyslexia who desperately need help, too." He held my hand, looked me in the eye, and started telling me what Hillary had done for exceptional children. I felt comfortable with this high-ranking public official. Even so, when a former president holds my hand and talks to me, do not expect me to remember what he says. Oh, wait. Aren't generalities and vagueness typical of politicians? Maybe that affected my recall.

The following year, 1971-72, our program more than doubled in size. We had to move to a larger donated facility. Parents began to bring their children for screening and to the weekly tutorial program from neighboring towns, sometimes driving as long as two hours one way. As parents from these nearby communities became experienced tutors, they wanted to establish their own programs. Our association worked with them in establishing satellite programs.

Without a strong board made up of community people as well as parents and without financial partners such as the United Way, many programs like ours do not last. As parents see their children become successful readers, they drop out of the program. There are no recruits to take their place, and the programs dissipate.

Some forty-two years after its beginning, our program continues. In 2008, our association president wrote in a newsletter:

> *The past two years have been very educational for me. The most amazing thing that I have learned is that if you have dyslexia and you live in this area, you are a very lucky person. What we have here in Hopkinsville is second to none. It is actually one of the best, if not the best, educational program in the country. I was under the assumption that these programs existed in most cities. I was wrong. The work that is being done through the screenings and tutorial programs is truly phenomenal. We have a terrific staff and wonderful volunteers who devote countless hours to make this Association a model for all others.* [30]

Part of the longevity of our program is due to our local United Way. We have never had any local tax money or state and federal assistance. In 2012, our allocation from United Way was around $18,000. We exist with business and individual donations, in-kind donations (such as use of facilities and a free accountant), and volunteers.

While we could not exist without United Way's help, we have not been as successful in seeking donations from individuals and businesses. Much of the public does not understand dyslexia until it touches a family member or close friend. Many believe that our school systems are, or should be, taking care of students with dyslexia. Dream on, my friends.

The picture is not all bleak. We have won some small grants, but they are time-consuming to write and with over-extended schedules, they often don't get written. In addition, many grants are restrictive in how the funds are applied, making them unsuitable.

Chapter 16
A Life-or-Death Situation

I firmly believe that deep in the soul, everyone has a champion that can overcome and do great things.

—Bruce Jenner, former Olympic Gold medalist, dyslexic

I recall a time when I helped with what could have been a life-or-death situation.

All tutors and students were working aloud in pairs in a classroom near the outside entrance of a small classroom. I did notice one student not fully cooperating, and I saw the supervisor giving him extra help. She came over to me and said, "Billy is having a bad day. He is fighting harder to keep from working than he is working."

The words were no sooner out of her mouth before her impulsive, upper-elementary-school student, bolted like a streak of lightening. He was outside before either of us could react. When my nerve impulses finally got the message to my brain, Billy was nowhere to be seen.

We were located in the middle of town between two busy streets. I went toward the front street. I could hear the cars swish up and down. It seemed that the street had never been so busy or the cars and trucks so fast. As I faced the street, a catholic church was to my left. A drive-through dry cleaner and Chevron station were to my right.

The supervisor caught sight of Billy and yelled, "There he is behind the cleaners."

"You take the back side and I'll go down the sidewalk," I yelled back. I wanted to keep him off that busy street. Billy happened to be one of our scholarship students whose parents were unable to tutor in the program.

I ran down the sidewalk with my heart racing both from physical exertion and adrenaline produced from a wild student running away in a rage. My shoe came off and I was left with one shoe—the other foot with only a stocking. There was no time to stop to get my shoe. My leg—in fact—my entire body was so numb from fear that I hardly felt the gravel or anything else under my feet. I kept moving. Billy had disappeared from my sight but I knew the supervisor was on his trail.

There he was on the service-station lot where cars were pulling in and out. One driver honked at him.

The attendant yelled, "Watch out, young man! You're going to get run over!"

With mouth open, I panted for more air. Just then, I saw a high woven fence that enclosed much of the park on the far side of the service station. The supervisor closed in on him on one side and I closed in on the other.

There was no way Billy could get over that eight-foot fence. That did not keep him from trying, though. We grabbed him as he screamed and kicked. Worn down from his attempted escape, he soon calmed down as we spoke to him gently and calmly.

He returned to school the next week, but we never again let him and his tutor work anywhere near an escape route.

I did retrieve my shoe—but only after Billy was safely on his way home.

The Locked Car

I recall another student with the same impulsive nature, dashing as fast as a speeding car from the tutoring room. Somehow, he had his mother's car keys. He locked himself in her car and refused to come out. We watched him because of safety issues. When he was ready to work again, he opened the car door and resumed his work. He had some overtime to do to make up for his self-imposed time-out.

After ten years, I had reached the burnout stage. By then we had another person who had the training and experience to supervise, but more and more administrative duties were thrust upon me. I was still the "buck stops here" person.

The Baptizing

On another occasion, I was not at the program but at home. As soon as I picked up the phone, I recognized our supervisor's voice and immediately sensed stress and even rage in her tone.

"Good grief. What tragedy has befallen us now?"I asked.

Susie, the supervisor managed to spit out, "Mr. Smith took J.C. to the water fountain, and before the entire group turned the fountain on and ducked J.C.'s head under it."

"Why?"

Susie, sounding a bit calmer, went on, "Mr. Smith had told J.C., his student, that if he had to tell him the meaning of a certain word one more time that he was going to duck his head under water."

"Why did Mr. Smith do something so ridiculous?"

Susie said, "He reminded me that I had told him earlier that if we made a promise to a student, we should always keep it."

"Horrors," I said, "I guess we did too good a job instilling consistency with the tutors and parents." My task was to reprimand, yet try not to offend an otherwise good tutor.

To make the situation worse, J.C. was the supervisor's son. While water may have cooled J.C.'s head, Susie's self-control helped keep her "cool" until she got home. Such unusual and inhumane treatment was inconsistent with our philosophy. We were firm but kind. We showed students respect and tried our utmost to build self-confidence and self-worth.

"Susie, I think we have a tutor with dyslexia. Do you remember the story I once told you about my student who understood everything literally? The one who thought he was to decorate a piece of clothing when I said *book jacket* instead of *book cover."*

Persons with dyslexia often understand things literally. Susie, a little less exasperated, said, "I guess the moral to this is: 'Be careful what you ask for.'"

Chapter 17
Bob's Story

We do not see things as they are, we see things as we are.

—Talmud

Bob began our program in the third grade, reading at a 1.3 grade level. [31] When he left the program in the seventh grade, he was reading at the ninth-grade level, two years above grade level. At that point, we gently encouraged Bob to leave the program. Even though he was still motivated to continue, we knew he could make it.

When Bob started with us, he was a behavior problem at school. He would become so frustrated at not being able to do his work; that he would often explode.

Standing several rooms away, I could hear and almost feel the vibrations of Mrs. Chandler's door as Bob slammed it with his mighty swing. The school secretary in the nearby office would shake her head and say, "I don't know how Mrs. Chandler puts up with him."

Not only did Bob provoke his gentle teacher, he verbally attacked classmates and other teachers who tried to soothe him.

On more than one occasion, I was flabbergasted as I heard a mouthful of foul language pour forth from the open door of Bob's room. Then I heard his teacher say, "I am going to wash your mouth out with soap." Just what my Mom or Dad threatened on a few occasions when my mouth was less than holy.

I suppose the teacher reconsidered her threat. I later saw her half drag him into the hallway and say to him, "I cannot have you talking like this in my class. You sit HERE." The hall was Bob's home away from home. What teacher could tolerate such a disruptive student? At the end of the year, teachers at the next level feared getting him in their class.

Bob and Our Tutorial Program

From grades three through six, Bob missed only two Saturdays of our program—once to attend a party for underprivileged children and once because he was ill. Association volunteers provided transportation. When it was my turn to pick up Bob for school, his neighborhood was quiet at 7:30 a.m. When I drove Bob home around noon, the community seemed to have come alive with animated people of all ages who smiled and waved.

There was clutter and junk in many yards and an abandoned house with broken windows. Streets were narrow. I had to maneuver to the right to keep from scraping a passing car if I met one.

When nearing Bob's house, I saw the white picket fence with a gate opening to a walkway. In warm weather, there would be vigorously growing green plants on the porch, some with vibrant blooms. Like a balding head of hair, there were some bare spots in the grass, probably due to a number of older trees blocking the sun.

Sometimes I could see a truck in the driveway. *I wonder why his dad can't bring Bob to the dyslexia program on Saturday mornings?* I never asked. By providing transportation, we were sure that Bob would get there. He was always up, dressed, and even seemed glad to see us. Bob's parents were not able to tutor in the program, and Bob attended on a scholarship.

While pre-tests and post-tests provide objective measures of success, perhaps the most significant indications of change are in attitude and feelings of self-worth. The following is a quote from a retired teacher, who was Bob's Sunday-school teacher:

> *I knew something had happened to Bob but until I saw him in the Saturday program, I didn't know what. At church, Bob's peers used to shun him, saying behind his back that he was retarded. Bob stayed to*

himself and was shy and retiring. Now other
children accept him. He mingles with them, is
more outgoing, and is one of the group.

Bob, the Speaker

When he was still in high school, I asked Bob to speak at a community forum about his struggles with reading. At first, he was reluctant. Finally, he said, "If you want me to, I will."

I gave Bob a ride to the event. When I got to his house, he was dressed in a dark suit, white shirt, and red tie. His shoes were as reflective as a mirror.

He was a poised, mannerly, and articulate young man as he talked openly about his feelings—before and after the program. "I used to feel so 'dumb' when I played those games in second grade in your class. Everyone always got more words right than I did. I felt nobody liked me and people picked fights with me. I know I tormented Mrs. Chambers."

I asked, "Bob, what made you change from that bitter, incensed student we saw in elementary school to what you have become today?"

Bob hesitated as if he was anxious to choose the right words, then said, "When I started reading, after going to your program, I knew I wasn't dumb, that I wasn't different. I started feeling like I was somebody, and other people stopped treating me like I was no good. "

Bob was ready to graduate from high school and had ambitious plans for his future. I felt he had the reading skills to make of himself whatever he chose. I voiced this to one of our program volunteers. He added, "Equally important, maybe more so, is how Bob feels about himself."

I never saw or heard from Bob for over twenty years. I knew that after graduation Bob had plans to leave the community and maybe join some branch of the military. Occasionally, I thought of him.

Twenty Years Later

During the summer of 2009, I read in the newspaper of the death of Bob's mother. I recognized her from the street address of Bob's home, which remained imprinted in my memory.

Here was my chance to see long-term results of our program. I phoned the funeral home. They knew nothing of Bob, but the director said he would pass along my message and phone number should he come in. I assumed that was one of those "get her off the phone and forget about her" ploys.

I had a commitment to participate in a weekend antique show out of town and I could not go to visitation or the funeral. I couldn't shake my disappointment at missing my one chance to see Bob. It was like a captivating book taken from me before the climax. As I left town with my Honda Civic chock-full of wares for the show, on impulse I drove to Bob's home.

Feeling like an intruder, I stayed clear of the barking dogs as I waited for someone to come outside. After introducing myself to an in-law, I was invited through the white picket fence and into the house. Although it was after lunchtime, the enticing smell of freshly baked bread filled the air. Bob's sister, Rosie, greeted me as if only a yesterday had ticked away. Bob was not at the house, but his sister's phone call quickly brought him home. Bob's round face was still youthful but he had grown tall, muscular, and as handsome as a young Sydney Poitier.

After expressing my condolences over the death of his mother, I asked Bob a question or two, and he began filling me in on the past twenty-plus years.

"I am now retired from the Navy but am working at a naval base in New Jersey. I have been all over the world, even the naval base at Guantanamo Bay, Cuba."

At that point, Rosie joined the conversation. "I used to do Bob's homework for him. Now he has been everywhere and the only place I've been is across the line to Tennessee."

I looked at Rosie and said, "Sounds like Bob has a debt he needs to pay, doesn't he?"

She smiled and let Bob continue.

"My duties involved a type of intelligence in which I used cryptic codes. I continue to do this type of work as a civilian retiree." Bob kept on telling me about his work. It was hard for me to understand what he did. I suppose our roles had reversed. Just as the student Bob had difficulty with the symbols which made words, I had difficulty understanding the technical phase of his work.

I heard a car stop outside and the dogs started to bark again. Rosie quickly quieted them. In walked an impeccably attired young woman who looked as if she might have just walked out of an executive suite.

Bob stopped talking abruptly and said, "This is my wife, Jessie."

Jessie was pleasant and cordial.

I took advantage of this break in conversation to ask Bob, "Bob, in all of your duties in the navy using symbols, has your reading problem in any way hindered you?"

Bob unhesitatingly answered with an emphatic "No."

Chapter 18
Endless Success Stories

If you can dream it, you can do it.

— Walt Disney (who struggled with reading)

Attending the Dyslexia Tutorial Program each Monday evening was not a hardship for Connie and her son, Joseph, who was in grade five. It was a lifestyle. Connie tells her story below:

> *We have been involved in the dyslexia program for three years. I know it has made the difference between Joseph's excelling in school and his absolute failure.*
>
> *When my family was forced to leave Louisville and that city's dyslexia program, we were willing to give up close to thirty-percent of our income in order to keep Joseph in a reputable program. Other programs would only help if he were failing in school.*
>
> *We wanted to keep him from failing.*

In the local tutorial program, modeled after the one in Louisville, Joseph was helped by many dedicated parent tutors and supervisors to reach his full potential. Because of the local program, we never had to put him in special classes, and he has never known what it is like to fail in school. He tests at least two years ahead of the state average and in some subjects is considered advanced. I know he could not have achieved this if it was not for our involvement in this program.

As a parent tutor, I get great satisfaction knowing that because of my efforts, another child is making it in school. I do not know of any other method that gets the results the one used in the local program does.

Not only have I seen this method (alphabetic-phonetic-structural-linguistic) make a difference in my son's life, I have seen it make a difference in my brother's life. Bobby also attended one of these programs with my mother. He now holds a master's degree in computer science from the University of Cincinnati. Like my son, he could not have made it if it had not been for the dedicated people involved in a dyslexia program.

Making the sacrifice of driving one-and-a-half hours each way to attend the tutorial program is the best investment we have ever made in the education and future success of our son.

In 2009, while working on this book, we received a follow-up report on Joseph.

His mother wrote:

> *Raising a dyslexic child is not always easy; but when they learn to be the best, as they were created to be, it is a remarkable sight. In 2007, he earned the highest award in Boy Scouts by becoming an Eagle Scout. In 2008, he graduated with honors from high school. He enrolled at the University of Evansville, where he majored in mechanical engineering. Currently, he is in England at the U. E. English campus, Harlaxton College.*

In July 2012, I received the following from a father:

> *Just thought you might remember my son. He went thru your program years ago in the 1980s. It helped him get thru his schooling all the way to a Ph. D at University of ____. He is teaching in college now. Thanks.*

At the 2005 International Dyslexia Association Conference in Denver, Colorado, Dr. Richard K. Olson,

Institute for Behavioral Genetics, University of Colorado at Boulder, a researcher, was one of the keynote speakers. After passionately talking for over an hour about new insights into the brain and how dyslexic persons learn, he concluded by saying with resounding urgency: "We must find a way to apply this research to teach persons with dyslexia at affordable costs."

In that room filled with hundreds of people, I wanted to stand up and shout, "We know how. Stop. Listen. Let us show you."

Mr. Collins (Left), Dr. Charles L. Shedd's assistant, and
Dr. Shedd at Berea College in 1970.

Frances Crocker from Alabama, Ruth's roommate at
the Reading Research Institute at Berea College, 1970.

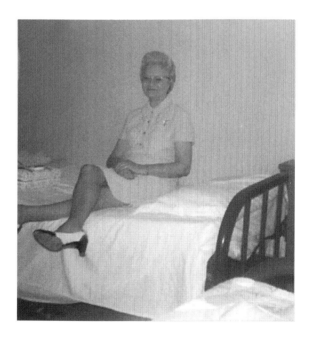

Joyce S. Pickering, Hum. D., Executive Director
Emerita,
Shelton School & Evaluation Center, in Dallas Texas.
This picture was taken at an
International Dyslexia Conference.

Student slides finger under print as tutor listens to her
read in our tutorial program.

Ruth and Linda Starr, Florida, at IDA conference
held in Chicago.

Ruth Lature and Dr. Sally Shaywitz, autographing her
book, *Overcoming Dylexia.*

Ruth entering the office of the
Dyslexia Association of the Pennyrile.

Ruth and Dom DeLuise, movie and television actor
and comedian. DeLuise was dyslexic.

Marcia Henry signing her book,
Dyslexia: Samuel T. Orton and His Legacy.

Stephen Cannell, a producer, of the TV series "The Rockford Files." He was a writer and a dyslexic.

Dr. Sylvia Richardson and Ruth Lature at the IDA
conference in Chicago, 2011. Dr. Richardson is a past
president of IDA and a pediatrician.

Mrs. Stephenson, a supervisor, helps tutor a student in
our tutorial program.

Author Tom West, Carolyn Weimer, and Ruth Lature
at an IDA conference in Philadelphia.

Board member Mike Bruce at the
Dyslexia Association's community education booth.

Director Ruth Lature supervising a dyslexia instructor and her student.

Left to right, front row: Steve Tribble, County Judge Executive and Dan Kemp, Mayor, with the dyslexia board signing a proclamation for October Dyslexia Awareness Month.

Left to right, back row: Connie Jones, Patsy Willis, Janice Cayce, Peggy Bozarth, Amy Nightingale, and Ruth Lature.

Governor Steve Beshear, Ruth Lature, and Janie Bruce
at the signing of Kentucky's House Bill 69, which
recognized dyslexia as a specific learning disability.

Trish Richardson, retired teacher, watches as a student
feels a word on the memory board.

Harvey Hubbell V, Ruth Lature, and Amy
Nightingale behind the poster of Hubbell's film
about dyslexia at the Chicago IDA conference.

The Wadlington family supports their daughter as she receives her award for perfect attendance at the tutorial program.

Susan Barton at an IDA conference. Susan developed a
method for teaching persons with dyslexia.

Betty Warner, Dyslexia Association of the Pennyrile
office assistant for ten years.

Bruce Jenner and Ruth Lature at an IDA conference.
Mr. Jenner won the gold medal for decathlon in the
Montreal 1976 Summer Olympics.

Ruth demonstrates the use of a memory board in a
staff meeting.

Ruth Lature and Henry Winkler—actor,
movie producer, author

Chapter 19
Adult Dyslexia

I never fight except against difficulties.

—Helen Keller

A few years before my retirement from the public school system, a colleague from one of our middle schools invited me to chat with her at a coffee shop. I arrived first, ordered my coffee black, and selected a table for two in a corner.

Jake

Beth arrived in her usual jubilant mood and bounced into a chair across from me.

"Well, you must be as addicted to coffee as ever. You couldn't wait for me," Beth blurted out half teasingly.

I quietly replied, "Better than the colored water you serve at your house," as I got up to get a cola for Beth.

Beth ranted on and on about the endless piles of papers she had to grade before school was out, ignoring me and letting the ice in her cola melt. Finally, I was able to get in a few words about the fantastic progress I was seeing in my first-graders.

With that, Beth changed the subject and said, "I know you worked with Jake years ago when you were at the reading clinic."

"Yes, for a brief time," I replied, wondering what brought this subject up. Jake was a highly competent math teacher at her middle school.

"Didn't you think that Jake was dyslexic when he came to you at the reading clinic?"

I ignored her question.

Beth went on talking. "Jake said that he didn't find out that he is dyslexic until graduate school."

Beth was not telling me anything that I did not already know. Jake's highly concerned parents brought him to me when he was in the primary grades. Jake was the youngest of five children and all of them had done extremely well in school. The parents questioned themselves, feeling alternately guilty and angry over Jake's reading problems. I did a reading evaluation.

I strongly suspected that Jake was dyslexic and urged his parents to take him to a psychologist. They refused. In those "dark ages," probably there was nothing to be gained from a psychological evaluation anyway. Few psychologists in the country were accurately detecting dyslexia back then.

His parents and I had many conversations. They knew as much about dyslexia as they were able to admit to themselves. I was qualified to notice the characteristics and suspect but not to diagnose. Jake did not attend our community dyslexia program. To his dad, dyslexia meant something was wrong with the brain. How could that be true when Jake was so smart? To so many parents and teachers, the person with dyslexia is just lazy or not interested.

In a recent interview, Jake told me he had done well in high school sports, but his dad thought sports interfered with his schoolwork. Being challenged academically because of his dyslexia, Jake said, "Sports were what kept me from dropping out of school. My dad never understood dyslexia and never admitted that it (dyslexia) was at the root of my problems at school."

In the past, Beth had seemed disinterested at the mere mention of dyslexia. I pressed her with, "Beth, what inspired your sudden interest in dyslexia?"

"You know those letters of intent we have to sign each spring?"

I nodded. There were three options on the letter of intent, issued from the superintendent's office, and we had to choose and sign one: to continue teaching, resign, or retire.

"Our principal, Mr. Randolph, discovered Jake had signed he was resigning. He sent his secretary to Jake's classroom with the document.

Before the secretary could fully explain, Jake frowned and said disgustedly, 'Oh, no. I've done it again.' "

Beth lowered her voice almost to a whisper. "Jake had meant to sign that he was returning but his reading problem caused Jake to sign in the wrong place. Mr. Randolph went to the superintendent, explained the situation, and secured another copy of the letter of intent. The matter was resolved before the paperwork went to the Board of Education."

Jake was fortunate to be among people who understood and accepted his dyslexia. I suppressed the rage that began to surface when I thought of all the "Jakes" of the world who must muster the grit to keep fighting their dyslexia day after day.

Before Beth hurried off, she said, "Jake has shared with me how painful it has been that he didn't discover his dyslexia until graduate school."

After Beth left, I got a hot cup of coffee and reflected. Apparently, as Jake grew older, his parents had never confronted him with the possibility of dyslexia. He should have known about this beast long before graduate school. Should I have tried to talk with Jake, a young boy in primary school, about what I suspected? I concluded that I should not have attempted to explain dyslexia to a second or third grade student when pediatricians, teachers, and even psychologists were denying its existence. I had no right to intercede where his parents chose not to tread. Does Jake blame me for not identifying his dyslexia? We may have that conversation yet.

The aroma of freshly perked coffee and the tantalizing lure of chocolate-chip cookies overwhelmed my self-doubts, at least temporarily.

Jake, as is true for persons with dyslexia in general, had to work harder for his education. While he was just as intelligent as his older siblings, who maintained top grades with ease, their achievements only added to Jake's stress and self-doubt. Often, creativity and perseverance lead to greater accomplishments for persons with dyslexia.

Jake has now retired from a successful coaching and teaching career and was ordained as a minister this year. He has been an eloquent lay speaker and pastor of a small church and now is a fully credentialed minister in the United Methodist Church, a denomination that has stiff requirements for its clergy.

Dr. Brown

In 2009, another Methodist minister came, as senior pastor, to one of the larger churches in our community. Since our part-time dyslexia office secretary, Betty Warner, attended his church, she wasted no time in telling me he was dyslexic. Betty had known dyslexic persons well, and I heard the excitement in her voice as she told me this. She must have surmised we had another person to join our crusade to help dyslexic persons.

We asked Dr. Brown to speak to the Board of Directors of the Dyslexia Association of the Pennyrile. His struggles and triumphs were as dramatic as any I had encountered in person or in reading. Here is a part of his story:

> *When I was seventeen years old and in high school, the principal told me I might as well drop out of school because I wasn't going to amount to anything. The teachers had never known what to do with me. I gladly took the principal's advice.*

He already had the attention of our board members as they sat stupefied. Dr. Brown continued.

> *I wanted to join the Air Force, but since I could not read and write, I failed the entrance exam again and again. I was finally accepted because young men were needed so badly during the war.*

This tall, muscular minister, now about sixty years old, neither looked nor acted like someone who had escaped deprivation in the back hills of Tennessee. Merrie, a board member entering late, ready to apologize for her tardiness, placed her hand over her mouth as she sensed the hushed silence. Dr. Brown gave a recognition wink and continued:

About a year into the Air Force, I met a superior officer whose wife knew how to help me. Every case of dyslexia is different, though. I never saw a word the same way twice. I applied highlighters of certain colors to certain words to standardize a word's appearance and to recall its sound and meaning.

Dr. Brown paused for questions.

In answer to one question, Dr. Brown stated he now has an undergraduate degree, a master's degree, and a doctorate. How fortunate to have been that wife and teacher. She completely turned a brilliant man's life around.

Robert

After retiring from full-time teaching, I did some private tutoring. A mother approached me about tutoring her son, who had just turned twenty. The son wanted to hide his inability to read; therefore, she could not persuade him to come to our community dyslexia program. He had finished his high-school work through adult education. He was granted a 504 accommodation so tests could be read to him.[32] I was amazed that anyone could achieve top scores while having even the math test read to him.

When his mother came to see me, she brought a stack of psychological evaluations done when he was much younger. The family had moved here from the northeast, where highly qualified psychologists and neurologists had done thorough work-ups. This very bright young man was on a second- to third-grade reading level. After meeting the student, I felt he had given up on himself even if his mother had not. Younger children in the family were doing well academically.

His mother did lots of research and was persistent. She visited the local office of vocational rehabilitation, whose personnel were not inclined to consider dyslexia a handicap. She challenged them, and the vocational-rehabilitation office agreed to pay me the hefty sum of $12.50 per hour to tutor her son.

Robert was working as a farm laborer from early morning to late at night. I agreed to see him at the office where I tutored him from seven to eight each morning, so he could get to his farm work. I saw Robert at this hour for two years. From his listless movements, his preoccupation (I often had to bring him back to the present), and his occasional closed eyes and head nodding, I concluded that he was sleep-deprived. Coming to tutoring was something he was pressed into doing.

I made quarterly reports to the vocational-rehabilitation office, stating objective data as well as my observations: nodding from sleep-deprivation, going through the steps of remediation without a trace of enthusiasm, coming late, etc.

I also made phone calls to his mother, telling her of my observations. Finally, we did get Robert to the fifth-grade reading level. At that point, his caseworker decided Robert must focus on a specific career goal. His goal was to be a licensed cross-country truck driver.

After his decision, we focused on road signs and signs in public places such as *private, elevator, danger, keep out,* and *construction zone*—all signs that one must read in order to function in the world. Robert went to a trucking school in the northwest. The last I heard, he had his own truck and was doing short transfer runs. Robert could have been remediated at an earlier age. What a tragedy.

Several books written by adults with dyslexia are included in the bibliography of this book. I have met some of these authors. These people became a success in life despite their dyslexia. Why did they become a success while other dyslexics succumb to this monster? I certainly do not have the answers—just some observations.

The "overcomers" persevered and were willing to work hard. Most came from families that encouraged and supported their student with dyslexia. Despite having teachers who did not understand, most had at least one teacher who believed in them and helped them believe in themselves.

Those whose parents could afford a private school for dyslexics had an advantage. In addition, dyslexia varies from mild to severe, making it much easier for the milder dyslexic to succeed.

Chapter 20
Struggles with Diagnosis

All labor that uplifts humanity has dignity and importance and should be undertaken with painstaking excellence.

—Dr. Martin Luther King, Jr.

In 1970, we had no school psychologists, psychometrists, or guidance counselors in elementary schools. As a public school teacher, I could refer students suspected of being dyslexic to the local mental-health center or to our community dyslexia program. As long as Dr. Shedd was alive, I trained and supervised people to do the screening tests. Dr. Shedd would interpret the tests and talk with parents when he came to do workshops. After he died in 1974, we continued with screenings and sent the tests to a psychologist.

Finally, Dr. Paul Thompson, a psychologist, moved to a nearby town. We solicited Dr. Thompson to help us evaluate students at the association. He continues to work with us today, doing monthly screenings at a nominal fee. How many of the clients who come to us could afford a full psychological evaluation at a cost of five-hundred to $2,800?

Our association provides scholarships, if need be, for the seventy-five to ninety dollars which Dr. Thompson charges. In addition, the psychologists whom I would recommend are in the larger cities. Some parents (perhaps dyslexic themselves), find driving in large cities difficult. Our local community college accepts Dr. Thompson's evaluation for student 504 plans.

Recently, a retired teacher phoned me. She wanted her grandson screened. A few years ago, we had screened her granddaughter. The family took her to a pediatrician who accepted Dr. Thompson's screening report and placed the granddaughter on medication for ADHD. The child's grandmother told me that the granddaughter had done extremely well in school. Had this teacher not called about her grandson, we would have never known how much we had helped through just screening. With our limited resources, both in time and finances, we cannot do a systematic follow-up on all students.

In the earlier years, I persuaded one parent to take his child for evaluation (unfortunately, to a psychologist who knew little about dyslexia). The parent came back saying, "I told you nothing was wrong with my child. He is just lazy."

Still another parent, who was a tiger to be reckoned with, got essentially the same report. This parent growled, "To tell me my child might be dyslexic was just like telling me my child has cancer!"

Today, I wonder if the father ever realized that the cause of his son's inability to read was not laziness, stupidity, poor teaching, or immaturity. Did he continue to deny there was a reading problem? As a young educator, I was downcast but steadfast.

The problem of getting an accurate diagnosis continues today. In 2006, I attended a regional meeting where state education officials came to gather input on the implementation of the revisions of the Individuals with Disability Education Act,[33] which President Bush signed into law in 2004. I asked school psychologists from a nearby county how they diagnosed dyslexia.

One young man dressed in a suit and tie answered, "We don't. Dyslexia cannot be defined. It is too elusive."

My startled reply was, "Oh, yes, dyslexia has been defined. I will show you."

I went to my car, picked up a binder of information compiled by the Tennessee Branch of the International Dyslexia Association, and took it to him. I opened the binder and showed him the definition of the International Dyslexia Association. He read the definition and said, "Oh, I guess dyslexia has been defined." I told him to keep the binder.

Was this young school psychologist at fault? He was functioning as a psychologist with what his higher education classes had taught him. Several years ago in the dark ages, I had a colleague tell me that dyslexia meant you could not learn to read. Unfortunately, some of that inaccurate, harmful, even absurd information is still floating around today.

Three years ago, a local school system was in the process of hiring a new superintendent. One of the questions put to the three finalists during a public forum was "What would you do, if chosen, for students with dyslexia?"

While I was out of town and did not hear him, a school-board member, upon my return, said, "Did you know Dr. Snow did not even know what dyslexia is? He could only stammer and stutter and seemed to have little or no comprehension of the term." This superintendent did not get the job.

Chapter 21
I Thought I Had Heard It All

It is an awful risky thing to live.

—Carl Rogers, author of *Client Centered Therapy*

Recently, I received a frantic phone call from our secretary, who functions as a receptionist when Dr. Thompson is screening. The quaking voice asked, "Can you come over to the church? I want you to hear with your own ears what a parent just told me."

I replied, "Yes, I will be there in ten minutes."

I took my partially eaten sandwich and grabbed my cola, eating my lunch as I drove. I kept asking myself, "What has happened now," as Betty gave me no clues. Upon my arrival, Betty said, "I want you to hear what this parent just told me."

I took the rather nervous young mother to a private area, offered to get her a drink from the vending machine, and asked if she would share with me what she had just discussed with Betty.

The previous day her second-grade son became agitated at school. According to the mother, the school had a "hands-off, no-tolerance policy." Apparently, that meant school officials called the police when a student became out of control. A school official contacted her and she got there quickly as she was nearby. At that point, she choked and had to pause before she could go on. I left her in private while I went to look for tissues.

When I returned, the mother was ready to go on. "When I saw my son, the police were already there and had him in handcuffs and shackles—my little seven-year-old boy."

On the inside, I was incensed but tried to maintain my role as an empathetic listener. However, I did let her know what the school did was very inappropriate, in my opinion. Although Dr. Thompson felt her son was severely dyslexic, dyslexia was not the only problem, and the mother was aware of this. The student had been seeing a psychiatrist. The child's mother immediately contacted the psychiatrist, who vehemently disagreed with the school's approach

I felt like saying to this mother (and maybe I should have), "I would go to the *Courier-Journal* or the *Lexington Herald*, the two most powerful newspapers in Kentucky, and spill my story. I would not go to a small-town newspaper where personnel may or may not believe you." The student's mother was not the type of person who would have been comfortable in taking my advice.

That evening Betty rang my phone again. She asked, "Did I really hear correctly? Did the police actually put this little boy in handcuffs and shackles?"

Unfortunately, I had to admit to Betty that what she had heard was true.

On April 18, 2012, I read a similar *Associated Press* article in our local newspaper. [34] However, this incident occurred in a small town near Atlanta, Georgia, and no reference was made to the kindergarten student's being dyslexic. The student threw a tantrum and was taken away in handcuffs, her arms behind her back.

As a retired teacher, I can see both the school's and the mother's viewpoints with the child I met. Yes, I would have been as incensed as that mother had been. On the other hand, when a child is out of control, he can hurt himself or others. If we improperly physically restrain him, there could be redness or bruising. Some inflamed parent could find issue and cause school officials to be reprimanded, sued, or possibly fired. We simply cannot let a child hurt himself or other students.

Nelson Lauver, the author of *Most Unlikely to Succeed* [35] talks about being isolated in a windowless safe with the door closed from the outside. Racing through his mind were the thoughts, "What if I get tired from lack of oxygen, fall asleep, and die?"

He goes on to write, "I fell into a deep sleep and had no idea if it was minutes or hours. I woke up in panic in the pitch black, not knowing where I was."

Such unbelievable cruelty happening in the 1960s makes me wonder how much suffering is inflicted because of the lack of understanding today.

In October, I read in a local newspaper that the Kentucky Board of Education recently passed a regulation that would keep school employees from secluding or restraining students. For this regulation to become effective, state legislation is required. The regulation stipulates that school personnel would have to train in other forms of discipline.[36] However, the regulation does not specify what these other methods should be. In my opinion, society has become so lax in its expectations of students, that the students lack respect for any authority.

What is the answer? From having worked a short time in a children's psychiatric hospital, I think each school should have a time-out room—a small room with a one-way mirror where someone can watch the student at all times. The room needs to be bare, with nothing with which the child can hurt himself. He needs to be treated kindly but firmly. The child should stay in this quiet, undisturbed situation until he gains control of himself. Now, there is a cry on the national level that any type of restraint or seclusion is abusive.

Second, at least one teacher in each school needs proper training on how to restrain a child. I witnessed a devoted special education teacher trained in behavior disorders sit on the floor and carefully restrain and calm an unruly student. At the same time, she continued her work with another student.

Third, if police are involved with young children, these dedicated people, who usually follow established procedures, need proper training and supervision.

My last and I think best idea is to teach students with dyslexia to read when they are young. Then they will have less frustration and, hopefully, little need to act out.

Homebound Work

After I retired, I did homebound work for a school system and was assigned a second-grade boy. This student had been in a behavior-disorders class, and sometimes restraint was necessary to control him. His mother objected to the restraint and managed to get him on homebound. This meant he had me for a total of two hours a week.

I had no training in behavior disorders and only managed to get the student to work ten of the thirty minutes we had together. Then he would start to shred his work or grab my records and refuse to return them.

I would have to chase him around the table to retrieve my papers. Finally, I bought a metal carrying case that I could close and lock.

If I left work for him to finish, even the little he had done in my presence was likely to be lost or destroyed when I returned. Rarely did he do any of my assignments.

An adult was required to be in the home when I was present. Where was his mother? She would go into another room and close the door, probably the only peaceful time she had.

What was the answer in this situation? I saw him alone; therefore, he was not a threat to other children. I accepted his verbal attacks as part of his disabilities. A behavior-modification system, which included rewards, was not effective. Was he being educated? No.

He and his mother soon moved to another state where she felt the educational system was better. I am not sure what she meant by *better*.

PART THREE

PUBLIC SCHOOLS

Chapter 22
Making a Difference

The probability that we may fail in the struggle ought not to deter us from the support of a cause we believe to be just.

—Abraham Lincoln

After the start-up of our community dyslexia program, my colleagues perceived me with mixed feelings. Some thought of me as an expert, while others were dyslexia skeptics.

I worked in public school systems for thirty-five years, retiring from full-time service in 1999. My interest in reading disabilities first began when I was doing student teaching in a middle school. My job was to teach English to seventh-graders who were slow readers. I found myself teaching more reading than English.

When I was hired as a seventh-grade reading teacher the next year in another school system, the principal, whose son had reading difficulties, thought seventh graders needed another year of reading.

Having had a wonderful learning experience the next summer at George Peabody College for Teachers, I boxed up the reading textbooks issued to me and brought a portion of the school library to my room. I let the students have a choice in what they read. Many of them became bookworms. For years, nearly each time I went to the public library, I would meet one of my former students.

I went from seventh-grade teacher to a reading-clinic teacher to an elementary-reading resource teacher, where I stayed for many years. Five years before I retired, my school system decided we could teach all children within a regular classroom. The principal assigned me to a first grade classroom. Some of my co-workers were betting that I would not make it through mid-year since I had never taught in a regular elementary classroom.

They lost their bet. I spent five magnificent years in that classroom. I brought to the regular classroom many of the techniques we used in our community dyslexia program. One teacher who thought I would not last half a year in first grade ended up saying, "She could teach a rock to read." Teachers at the next level wanted my former students in their classroom because they knew they were getting students who could read.

I taught everything possible with a game. I invented many of the games, some of which were published and are available commercially. For my less able students, I threw the prescribed reading books in a box and let them collect dust. I used the Merrill Linguistic Readers,[37] which have a controlled vocabulary.[38] I taught phonics not in isolation but in application as I had students decode.[39] A crucial step for a student with dyslexia is to be taught to *use* phonics with practice, drill, and repetition, varying the routine as much as possible. The more able readers soon transitioned to the adopted reading series.[40]

Through the years, I observed that most textbooks and workbooks taught words by sight. This means remembering the word from the way it looks. Phonics, syllabication, suffixes and prefixes came later.

This never made any sense to me. I thought the purpose of phonics, syllabication, and other word attack skills was to help students decode words. If the student already knew the words, then he had little use for these word-attack skills. It seemed to me that reading was taught in reverse.

Since I now had a heterogeneous classroom, some students needed the language-experience approach. One of the most exciting times for the students and me was sitting on the carpeted floor and making books come alive.

First graders wanted to sit close to me and rub my arm or feel the smoothness of my hose. We must foster the love of reading in all children.

I started teaching first grade with self-doubts but with grit and determination, honed by the trials of the reading institute years ago at Berea, I fully experience being a teacher.

Chapter 23
Tough People Survive Tough Times

It is not what administrators do not know; it is what they presume to know that hurts us.

—Anonymous

In the beginning, special education was perceived as education for those of low intelligence. The term learning disability (LD) seeped into our school system. By then, we had one psychometrist for every 10,000 students. As a resource teacher and later as a first-grade teacher, I referred an occasional student for psychological testing to determine if he qualified for a special class.

Dyslexia was in my vocabulary, but the word was not used officially. Shockingly, in some school systems today, teachers are not supposed to use the word *dyslexia.*

Getting someone placed in a class was often close to a year-long process. It took at least a month with a new student to determine if a referral was necessary.

The referral process took at least one meeting because the parent had to give permission for the testing. There was a wait for testing, a wait for results, and a wait for meetings with parents and specified school personnel.

Placement

The parent, classroom teacher, psychologist or psychometrist,[41] and special education teacher usually made up the Admissions and Release Committee (ARC).[42] The purpose of this committee was to consider all factors regarding the student, especially classroom performance. We always placed our students based on their test scores obtained by the psychometrist or psychologist. What was the purpose of the meeting? I often learned whether a student would receive help in a hallway discussion before meeting with the parents.

To receive the help, the student had to have a specific point spread between his IQ score and his achievement-test score. The number of points varied from state to state. This is called the *discrepancy formula*.[43] Therefore, a student might qualify in one state, move to another, and be out of special education.

If the student had the required point difference between achievement scores and intelligence scores set by the state, he was eligible for special education. If he qualified, an individual-education plan, called an IEP, [44] would be written at this meeting. Sometimes the IEP was prepared before the meeting, which gave the parent little or no input in the student's achievement goals, methods of evaluation, or duration of instruction.

In my opinion, the procedure was an unfair numbers game. Human beings are human beings and can't be reduced to numbers. Ideally, I wanted to put a name to the student's academic difficulties, which would give the parents and teachers an understanding of why the child was struggling. Then school personnel would be in a better position to correct the problem. I could only suggest that the student might be dyslexic and articulate some of the characteristics that led to my suspicion.

It did not make a great deal of difference whether the student qualified or not. If he was dyslexic, he probably would not be taught by a research-based method, nor would the special education teacher have an appreciable working knowledge of dyslexia. Instead, he would be placed in a class with the mentally retarded and taught out of a lower-level textbook. Even today, if you are a special education teacher or a reading specialist, these titles do not mean you are trained to teach students with dyslexia.

Sally Shaywitz, in her classic book, *Overcoming Dyslexia*, says the following:

> *Has anyone evaluated the effectiveness of public school programs generally used to*

teach reading to dyslexic students? Yes, and in general, public school programs for children with reading disabilities are failures. The designation "special education" per se is insufficient. The evidence is overwhelming. One study that examined children's reading before and after they spent three years in a resource room as part of special education found no change in word reading scores relative to their peers and a significant decline in their performance on measures of reading comprehension.[45]

Still, I fought for placement when there was an obvious reading disability. I felt the student could get more attention in a small group than I could give in a larger class. If the student was a behavior problem, the special education teacher could best cope with that in a small group. Special education classes helped mildly dyslexic students but were not the solution.

Through attending workshops and conferences, such as the International Dyslexia Association conference, reading, and talking with highly accomplished people such as Dr. Shaywitz, I became convinced that ARC meetings were unproductive.

I left most ARC meetings seething with suppressed anger after dealing with professionals who had power over me but either ignored the facts or lacked the information to make decisions in the best interest of the child.

Most principals, guidance counselors, psychologists, and teachers were trying to work within a system that denied even the existence of dyslexia.

Blame serves no useful purpose unless it can affect change.

Help—I'm in Trouble

My yearly evaluations as a teacher from my supervisors had always been exemplary. Moreover, as retirement time grew closer, I really did not care if my evaluations were perfect. I became more assertive. Sometimes the psychologist chose the wrong test. When a student gets no answers correct on a subtest yet he scores on grade level, the test range is not low enough to measure what he knows or does not know. He earned his scores by guessing. I began to point out such flaws. I "bucked" the system.

One particular student is very vivid in my memory. He enrolled in my first-grade room late in the year. Luckily, I was able to get him evaluated by the school psychologist. I had already heard in the hallway that he did not qualify for help.

The school psychologist, guidance counselor, special education teacher, principal, and I all crowded into the principal's windowless office. The parents did not come. Each of us had a copy of the psychologist's report. The young, buoyant psychologist shuffled her papers and began rapidly interpreting the results of her tests. The principal seemed to be gazing at a list on his desk. The special education teacher and guidance counselor commented on their observations of Jay in my classroom.

> *Jay was on-task, then not on-task. He never volunteered to participate in classroom discussion and failed to focus on the teacher when she gave instructions. He squirmed in his seat and stared out the window when others were working....*

The psychologist concluded, "Jay reads on grade level and does not qualify for special education."

With that pronouncement, the special education teacher passed previously prepared paperwork to the principal for his signature.

I interjected, "This child can read six words on beginning first grade level. Are you saying he is on grade level when we are near the end of first grade?" I looked straight at her.

"Oh, yes, Mrs. Lature," the physiologist said. "As I said, he is reading at 1.8 (first grade, eighth month)."

When I had her give me the subtest scores, she reported that on most of the subtests, Jay had read all items incorrectly.

Tense and angry, I managed to say to the psychologist, "If Jay managed to get nothing correct on the subtests, he obtained his score by guessing. You chose the wrong test. The basal [46] was not low enough. I know what this child can and cannot do. I work with him every day."

I had threatened her authority. Her cheeks turned a beet red. All participants in the meeting became more alert. I continued.

"The purpose of our coming together is to decide what is best for Jay," I managed to get out haltingly. "He needs more help than I can give him in a classroom of twenty-six other students. What is going to happen to him next year?"

I was flustered and having trouble expressing myself. The psychologist fumed, "Miss Lature, you have a retrieval problem." I felt the pierce of a dagger but was too frozen to respond.

Some of the committee members had already signed the paperwork, agreeing that Jay did not have the discrepancy between his average intelligence and his achievement level to qualify for help.

When Mr. Flexner, the principal, passed the paperwork to me, I said, "I cannot sign this because I am not in agreement with the decision of this committee."

"You are not signing that you agree with the committee. You are just signing that you were in attendance." I was skeptical.

With his insistence, I finally signed the paper but wrote in my own handwriting, "I do not agree with the decision of the ARC committee." This scenario was repeated a number of times in other ARC meetings.

After the evaluation, Jay was rather subdued on the overt level. However, I found feces smeared on the wall of my room—the first and only time in my career. Some first-graders like to tattle, so I gently confronted Jay. Without a lot of interrogation, he admitted the misdemeanor. Did I punish him? No. But, I made him clean the wall.

This precious child had suffered enough in someone's classroom from trying and failing, probably being ridiculed by his classmates and likely having no child or adult for a friend. His dad was already in prison and his mother was facing charges, too.

Soon after Jay's ARC committee meeting, the principal placed a written reprimand in my personnel folder. At that point, I had taught thirty-plus years and this was the first blight on my record.

The reprimand cited a remark I had made to another teacher regarding Jay's situation about a week prior to the ARC meeting. I was guilty of saying to one or two teachers that the committee was not going to help Jay.

Since his mother had been to school to talk with me and subsequently failed to attend the ARC meeting, the principal assumed, wrongly, that I had told Jay's mother to stay away from the meeting.

I took the reprimand hard. As soon as I escorted my students to the buses, I pattered down the long hallway to the principal's office. I had composed myself enough that I thought I could talk without bursting into tears. The principal invited me in and closed the door, which further darkened the cluttered room and my somber mood. My hurt must have shown on my face, because the principal was gentle and kind, almost apologetic.

Amid the muffled roar in the reception area, he said, "Telling the mother to stay away was unprofessional. Until now, I've had the utmost regard for your professionalism."

"I agree that, if I had done what you are accusing me of, I would have acted unprofessionally."

Verdict—guilty as charged.

He opened his office door for me, and I parted with my head held low like the old collie dog of my childhood after he had received a scolding.

When I reached home, I found sanctuary in the quietness of my bedroom. The sweetened iced tea quenched my thirst but not the rumblings of my mind. I reasoned, *Mr. Flexner reprimanded me not solely on his own accord but from pressure and fear of those higher in authority.* I had become too much of an advocate for children with dyslexia. Did the principal feel forced against his will in order to retain his job, to avoid a lawsuit, or to maintain the approval of colleagues?

There is limited freedom unless one has the courage to stand alone—I did.

What happened to Jay? School was soon out and I never saw him again. I wondered if his dad was in prison because he could not read. Had his reading disability blocked his path to success to the extent that he drifted into drugs to *feel good*?

Help—I'm in Trouble Again

Sometime later I received the second reprimand of my career. It read:

> *Please be very careful about putting into writing your feelings concerning the possibility of a child's being ADHD. This could be very costly to us.*
>
> *Remember the referral process is designed to help us determine the needs of the child. One of these needs could be medication for ADHD, but this problem must be diagnosed by a certified child psychologist and medication prescribed by a physician.*
>
> *The information gathered during the referral process should identify a student as potentially ADHD. It is then the parent's responsibility to decide if a doctor is to be consulted.*
>
> *School personnel must be very careful not to diagnose these problems, as we try to provide*

parents with feedback about inappropriate behavior.

I certainly agree in theory. If one carefully compares what I wrote with the principal's admonition, he is not comprehending and directly relating to what I had said:

To Whom It May Concern:

_____ has been in my ungraded primary class since ____. From the beginning, he has been unable to focus and follow group instructions. Although he has a study carrel for special-needs children, he rarely sits. He is often seeing what someone else is doing, crawling under his desk, interrupting me rather than raising his hand and waiting his turn.

He is motivated and is very pleased with himself when he does well. He is doing quite well in math, is only now beginning to read three letter words, rarely gets any of his spelling correct, and cannot get his thoughts on paper in a complete sentence. He has fine motor and spatial problems. Overall, he is one of my weakest students despite the fact that an AmeriCorps worker has been able to give him one-to-one help. He is not a mischievous child; he just cannot stay focused.

I see symptoms of ADHD and feel that it would certainly be in his best interest to have him evaluated for this possibility.

I tried. Where is this child today? Did he impulsively run in front of a car? Is he on a welfare roll or in prison? Is he living a meager existence with a menial job?

When I received this notice, I was boiling. A pot of boiling water must bubble and escape, I usually tried to keep the lid on, but doing so makes for taut nerves and tight muscles.

Reflection

One of life's lessons is that if we feel unjustly treated, defeated in our attempts and oppressed, we can, with God's help, turn injustice, defeat, and oppression into something positive. The choice is ours.

Chapter 24

And the Beat Goes On...

When you are wrestling with a gorilla, you don't stop when you are tired; you stop when the gorilla is tired.

—Robert Strauss

It has been thirteen years since I retired as a public school teacher. However, the battles continue. Yesterday, I walked out of a school—exhausted, angry, and in turmoil. Voluntarily, I had accompanied the parents of a dyslexic and ADHD student to a school meeting to decide if their son should repeat first grade. School officials had told the parents they had no voice in the school's decision.

To retain or not to retain was not my issue, although I am aware that substantial research proves retention is not the best solution.[47] I attended the meeting as an advocate—to help ensure the parents' rights were not violated.

Sadly, I was unsuccessful. The parents were not satisfied with the screening done by the school psychologist. They were told the school system would not do a full evaluation. According to Federal Law,

IDEA 2004, even if an evaluation is done by the school system, if the parents are not satisfied, they can request another evaluation at the school system's expense.

Today, I meet parents who tell me they have asked to have their child retained and their request was denied.

In the last three years, locally, we have gone from "this child has to be retained" to "no, your child cannot be retained." Operating under federal legislation called *No Child Left Behind*, education has flipped-flopped. Why not let the parents decide what is best for their child if educators cannot? I know *No Child Left Behind* is a program where all children succeed, but is this really happening?

Unfortunately, the student with dyslexia is often left behind.

Chapter 25

Who Is Accountable?

Hard work doesn't guarantee success but improves its chances.

— B J Gupta

In our office, we field many phone calls from distraught parents trying to find help for their dyslexic child. The call below is typical:

> *My son was diagnosed with dyslexia and is receiving no help from school. The principal says our state does not recognize dyslexia. Therefore, the law does not require the school to have a specially trained teacher to teach him. I cannot find (or afford) a private tutor. What do I do?*

That parent needs to know that the Federal Special Education Law, called the Individuals with Disabilities Education Act (IDEA) has a definition of specific learning disability, which includes dyslexia.

Another parent shared this story.

When my child was in elementary school it was a nightmare. The teachers didn't know what dyslexia was, and the school psychologist told us dyslexia was a rare eye disorder. He was finally tested at _____ Hospital and was diagnosed him with dyslexia, dysgraphia and central auditory processing disorder, and the school psychologist still wanted to argue over the diagnosis. He is being tutored at_____Center and they teach him Orton-Gillingham. The _____ Center and _____ Hospital have each been a life saver.

I share part of another e-mail.

We spent 1000s [sic] of dollars to have our child tested because the school found nothing wrong...however, going into fifth grade his reading level was at 1.8 —some of the areas of the test he didn't even measure they were so low... My child could do everything and made average to above average grades but could not read a lick. [sic]

IDEA demands that every school in every city in every state provide a "free and appropriate" education for all children with special needs, including dyslexia. If the student's dyslexia is not severe enough to have a significant negative effect on his learning, then the school does not have to provide services. School systems may say the child is doing well enough when he really is not.

If the student truly does not qualify under IDEA, there is another Federal Law (Section 504 of the Rehabilitation Act) that guarantees that he is not treated with prejudice because of his disability. This child might get help under a 504 plan.

A few weeks ago, I received the following e-mail written by a desperate mother:

> *I'm a mother of a son whose been diagnosed with auditory dyslexia and no one in our school system is qualified or familiar with this I am at the end of my rope my child has been tested by dr _____ in l'ville he scored very high on iq scores he's in 3rd grade but on a 1st grade reading level his self-esteem is very low when it comes to reading even thou we praise him al the time. do you all offer classes or tutoring I live in _____ county and I'm willing to do just about anything do get help Your reply would be appreciated thank you [sic]*

I know the psychologist who diagnosed her child and consider him to be highly qualified to make this diagnosis. Can school officials be held accountable for not educating her dyslexic student? Yes. Apparently, neither the mother nor the school system knows that. Parents frequently tell me that school officials report having no one on staff trained to teach a dyslexic. In that case, the law obligates the school to go outside the school system to secure services. I hope that the situation is improving. Parents often have blind faith in school personnel, and many are so intimidated that they don't dare question a school official.

Accountability is not simple. Today, many compassionate, dedicated elementary and secondary teachers are distraught over their inability to teach their students with dyslexia. When their students do not achieve, most teachers are bewildered, confused, and frustrated. While mildly dyslexic children may excel in a supportive, regular classroom, a teacher trained in teaching students with severe dyslexia should work with those students. The classroom teacher should not feel guilty because she cannot meet their needs.

Parents and Teachers

In some cases, a student's parents may know more about dyslexia than the student's teacher. Depending on the personality of the teacher and the parents' approach, this can create a teacher/parent conflict.

Some educators still question the existence of dyslexia and hold stubbornly to the belief that the student is obstinate, lazy, undisciplined, immature, spoiled, or lacking in intelligence. Dyslexia appears to be a well-kept secret.

Teaching Methods

Few colleges and universities are teaching educators how to recognize dyslexia much less address the issue of how to teach students with dyslexia.

The International Multisensory Structured Language Education Council (IMSLEC, the accrediting arm of the International Dyslexia Association established in 1995) lists methods appropriate for persons with dyslexia and training sites. While that list may not be exhaustive, it is imperative to establish criteria for researched, effective methods. Otherwise, anyone could advertise as a dyslexia tutor and charge exorbitant amounts of money to unsuspecting parents.

Once faith or confidence in a method is established and progress is not made, the student and parents feel more discouraged and hopeless.

I have seen appropriate methods fail because of sporadic attendance and research-based materials used with too little teacher/tutor training and adherence to procedure.

Through the years, we have let textbook companies play too much of a role in setting our curriculum. Do we need that costly glossy paper for persons with dyslexia? Do we need all those enticing, colorful pictures? The slick paper and vividly colored pictures add tremendously to the cost. Wouldn't this money be better spent on effectively trained teacher helpers?

In beginning reading, we are often not teaching through word-reading. Instead, we are teaching *picture reading*. The student looks at the pictures and recalls words and story content from pictures. Ask the student a word in isolation and see if he knows it.

A few years ago at an International Dyslexia Association conference, a community group spoke of taking on a *watchdog* role on how students with dyslexia were taught. Texas, the state that had the first and most comprehensive law, shared a statistic with our group: out of approximately ten-thousand students, only ten students were identified as dyslexics. This means that many students who have dyslexia are never identified.

According to most national organizations, ten percent of the population has dyslexia. Therefore, the system was failing to serve 990 of its students. Furthermore, the system's idea of remediation was to put these students, unattended, with a computer program for forty-five minutes per week. This was a way of skirting the law and giving token teaching. At best, remediation takes time and much effort. There is no quick fix.

Chapter 26
The Debate

My grandfather once told me that there were two kinds of people: those who do the work and those who take the credit. He told me to try to be in the first group. There was much less competition.

— Indira Gandhi

For years, people in higher education have argued over such issues as labeling the reading problem as a *disability* or a *disorder*, or even if we should use a label at all.

While the "experts" were debating, we were teaching these students in our community program to read, and that is what matters.

In recent years, major magazines such as *Time*, *Newsweek*, and *Fortune* have splashed *dyslexia* across their front covers. Congress has recognized the term, dyslexia as a subtype of specific-learning disability since the passage of Public Law-142 in 1975. Yet some thirty-seven years later, parents still tell me that their principal or teachers say their state does not recognize dyslexia, does not test for dyslexia, and does not have properly trained teachers to teach dyslexic children.

The Blame Game

Playing the blame game is of no value; however, trying to analyze and evaluate for correction does help. Teacher-training institutions need comprehensive programs so teachers can be educated to teach our dyslexic children. What can you expect other than denial from elementary and secondary teachers when they are told there is no such thing as dyslexia?

These leaders in education need to go into the research labs in places like Yale and Tufts universities and look at the comparison between a dyslexic's brain and a normal reader's brain. With fMRIs, a wealth of information has been uncovered.

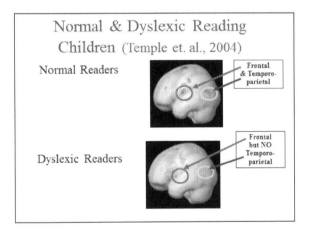

Normal & Dyslexic Reading Children (Temple et. al., 2004)

Normal Readers — Frontal & Temporo-parietal

Dyslexic Readers — Frontal but NO Temporo-parietal

Used by permission of Elsie Temple, Dartmouth College.

One of the mountaintop experiences of my career was visiting the dyslexia-research center at Beth-Israel

Hospital in Boston. Dr. Gordon Sherman started documenting changes in the brain as early as 1970.

I shall always remember a question Dr. Sherman asked: "If there was a way to surgically remove or otherwise eradicate dyslexia, would we really want to?" He went on to expand on how talented and creative persons with dyslexia are and then ask, "By ridding the individual of dyslexia, would we also destroy their creativity?"

Years later, more and more discoveries were made regarding hidden talents of persons with dyslexia. Drs. Brock and Brock have captured those often hidden gifts in their recent book, *The Dyslexic Advantage*.[48]

Two years ago, I asked the mother of one of our former students how her son was doing. He had really struggled in our tutorial program. The family could not afford a private school. Her face glowed as she said, "He is a millionaire. He makes more money than all four of my non-dyslexic children combined." He was a successful businessperson.

Many of our leaders are dyslexics. Three governors come to mind. Mississippi's Governor Phil Bryant,[49] Connecticut's Governor Dan Malloy,[50] and Vermont's Governor Peter E. Shumlin [51] overcame dyslexia.

Governor Bryant was in fourth grade before a knowledgeable teacher discovered his dyslexia. During the dyslexia bill signing in Mississippi, Gov. Bryant, age fifty-seven, said, "I repeated the third grade. What a difficult, horrible experience that was for a young child."

Governor Dan Mallory spoke at the end of the school year to students at Eagle Hill School in Greenwich telling students, "I'm the governor of the state of Connecticut, and I can't write anything very well. It would be a long and laborious process to even write a sentence."

At another school by the same name in Hardwick, Connecticut, Vermont's Governor Shumlin spoke at commencement telling students about an incident when he was in second grade. The principal called him out of class to join a conference with his parents. According to the Governor, the principal told his parents, "We don't know what's wrong with this kid; we know he's not going to college, he's not going to have a profession." What changed this Governor's life? A young teacher took an interest in him and spent the next year teaching him to read.

Other Obstacles

I believe another obstacle has been the American Psychiatric Association's failure to use "dyslexia" as a diagnostic entity in its *Diagnostic and Statistical Manual of Mental Disorders*. This is the psychologist and psychiatrist's bible. Supposedly, the manual lists all known disorders and the criteria that must be present for a diagnosis. To confuse matters further, this association uses Developmental Reading Disorder. Remember, in federal law, dyslexia is listed under specific-learning disabilities. Would you think of Developmental Reading Disorder as dyslexia unless someone explained this to you? I have voiced my concerns to both the International Dyslexia Association and the American Psychiatric Association.

At several International Dyslexia Association conferences, I articulated my concerns to the president of the association and the directors. Usually their answers reflected that the American Psychiatric Association was a "tough" organization to deal with.

In 2002, I wrote the following letter to Harley A. Tomey II, who was then president of the International Dyslexia Association:

Dear Mr. Tomey:

I am a teacher with more than thirty years of experience in the area of dyslexia. I have a continuing concern with which I feel the Board of Directors of IDA can help. The fact that "dyslexia" is not used in the American Psychiatric Association's Diagnostic and Statistical Manual creates major problems.

Most psychologists, when diagnosing this learning difference, cannot or will not use "dyslexia" even though IDA clearly established a definition in 1994.

The educational term in most states, including my own, is "learning disability" which, as you know, includes a number of disabilities. As a result, a hodge-podge of instructional approaches are used in the name of helping dyslexic persons.... As we know, the dyslexic must be taught differently. The major teaching approaches have been identified by IMSLEC, the accrediting arm of IDA.

Until psychological examiners state in their reports that a student is dyslexic, a specific multisensory approach is not likely to be used. As long as we can deny that dyslexia exists, school systems can get by without providing appropriate remediation....

Therefore, I urge the powerful IDA board to work with the American Psychiatric Association to change its nomenclature in its next edition and include the term dyslexia.

In July 2006, I wrote the following letter to the American Psychiatric Association:

Dear Editor:

I am a semi-retired reading specialist with thirty-five years of full-time teaching experience. I have a master's degree in both education and psychology.

The purpose of this letter is to encourage you to place 'dyslexia' as a separate diagnostic entity in the next revision of your Diagnostic and Statistical Manual.

While dyslexia seems to be accepted and understood among the public (see cover stories in "Time," "Newsweek," "Fortune," and other magazines in recent years), there continues to be denial and confusion among professionals. This prevents the victims from getting appropriate help—so desperately needed. If we can deny something exists, we are relieved of the obligation of doing something about it. I am enclosing an e-mail our office received last month illustrative of this denial. A diagnosis of dyslexia necessitates a method of teaching that has certain characteristics. Many educators fear having to spend more money.

How many psychologists and educators have I heard say, 'Dyslexia doesn't exist because it cannot be defined?' For an answer, look to the International Dyslexia Association, National Center for Learning Disabilities, or the National Institutes of Child Health and Human Development which have essentially the same definitions.

> *While dyslexia can be defined, for purposes of the DSM, thinking in terms of characteristics of the disability would be more practical. Do what you have done with ADHD, depression, etc. List the major characteristics and designate which must be present (and to what degree) before a diagnosis can be made....*
>
> *Adding dyslexia to the DSM would greatly help dyslexics reach their full potential.*

In 1994, readers were invited to submit questions to the International Dyslexia Association's quarterly publication, *Perspectives*. My question was: "Since the term *dyslexia* is commonly used to refer to a learning difference in reading, why does the American Psychiatric Association NOT include *dyslexia* as a diagnostic entity in its nomenclature?"

Dr. Harold Lubin,[52] psychiatrist from New Jersey, answered my question in the Winter 1994 issue of *Perspectives*. He said:

> *In the "Diagnostic and Statistical Manual of Mental Disorders," (third edition-revised) the official classification of the American Psychiatric Association, the following definition is given: 'Developmental Reading Disorder - The essential feature of this disorder is marked impairment in the development of word-recognition skills and reading*

comprehension that is not explainable by Mental Retardation or inadequate schooling and that is not due to a visual or hearing defect or a neurological disorder.'

The diagnosis is made only if this impairment significantly interferes with academic achievement or with activities of daily living that requires reading skills.

He goes on to say:

Oral reading is characterized by omissions, distortions, and substitutions of words and by slow, halting reading. Reading comprehension is also affected. This disorder has been referred to as 'dyslexia. '

Dr. Lubin's quote gives an excellent description of dyslexia. Of course, if a student has difficulty with word recognition (decoding), comprehension will be affected.

Quoting him further, he says: "Thus, the APA is using Developmental Reading Disorder as synonymous with dyslexia. As we all know, professionals in the field, from all disciplines, are agonizing over a definition of dyslexia, and this is still in a state of flux. Hopefully this will be satisfactorily resolved." From 1994 to 2012—eighteen years—and we are still waiting.

Many of the conditions in the *APA Diagnostic and Statistical Manual* are diagnosed by listing significant characteristics of the condition. Then the manual states that a certain number must be present to a degree that markedly *interferes* with work, academics, etc., before a diagnosis is made.

Could a diagnosis of dyslexia be dealt with the same way? Diagnosing many medical disorders progresses along a continuum—for example, a patient's total cholesterol should be below two-hundred. What if his cholesterol is 201? Does he have high cholesterol? The diagnosis is made based on an arbitrary cutoff.

Sally Shaywitz, author of the highly recognized book, *Overcoming Dyslexia*, says, "The diagnosis of dyslexia is as precise and scientifically informed as almost any diagnosis in medicine.... In fact, there are times when I wish other diagnoses in medicine could be made with the same degree of precision."[53]

Many people argue that labeling a person with dyslexia is unhealthy and that damage can be done to his self-worth. Greater harm will be done to the person's feelings toward self if dyslexia is left undiagnosed and thus untreated.

My experience has been one of extreme relief on the part of older students, adult dyslexics, and parents of dyslexics when a name is finally put to their condition. I once worked with a family where the father of the dyslexic was deeply troubled because he had been playing with his son as a baby and dropped him.

This father had been unable to forgive himself because he thought accidentally dropping his baby had caused the reading problem. Imagine the relief when he finally forgave himself of this blame.

This relief also occurs in young children, but they are not able to articulate it as well. Often when a child has struggled and is finally diagnosed (he has a condition with a name), a parent breaths a huge sigh of relief, "Oh, that was my problem when I was in school. I was not dumb, stupid, and different."

Read some of the books written today by the *overcomers* who endured and are putting their feelings on paper. Those horrible names that they called themselves, and internalized, were false. This helps change the damaging feelings that dyslexics have harbored for years.

Chapter 27

Effects of Dyslexia

When I give, I give myself.

—Walt Whitman

D r. Sally Shaywitz says, "Just as a virus courses through tissues and organs, dyslexia can infiltrate every aspect of life."

Bruce Jenner, Olympic gold-medal winner, has said, "The biggest problem with dyslexic kids is not the perceptual problem; it is their perception of themselves. That was my biggest problem."

Dyslexia is real. A sympathetic teacher told me about a child who, in order to escape reading, would force his fingers down his throat before his daily reading class. He would vomit and be excused from that day's lesson.

My Experience

While not dyslexic, I can relate to this student's torture. In primary school, I had what would be diagnosed today as separation anxiety or social phobia.

School was a hostile world which no adult understood. To avoid a day of school, I once swallowed a fly as I heard that doing so would make me vomit. If I vomited, I was too sick for school. My experiment proved that swallowing a fly does not cause one to vomit. Because of my disabilities, I suffered for years with self-hatred, feeling different, and guilt for disappointing my parents—just as a dyslexic agonizes over his inability to learn to read.

Dyslexia—No Respecter of Persons

Until recently, we thought more boys than girls were dyslexic. However, research now shows the boy/girl ratio to be about equal. Boys tend to *act out* more and clown around whereas girls are quieter and more retiring. Thus, boys demand more attention and their reading problems are more likely to be observed.

The prevalence of dyslexia has no correlation with socio-economic levels. The less affluent are more easily intimidated, have less knowledge, and may not take full advantage of available resources. Therefore, they are more in need of advocates. In addition, when I taught in the public school system, nearly seventy-percent of my students fell below the poverty level as revealed through free and reduced-lunch applications. On the other hand, in our community we had families with the finances to afford a $20,000 to $40,000 private school (even $60,000 per year for a boarding school) for their children with dyslexia. These families often left our community in order to live near that private school. Dyslexic persons can learn to read commensurate with their ability. Last week, I read *The Cost of Literacy: Overcoming Learning Disabilities.*[54] The article is about a family in Chicago with a dyslexic child. The dad is a lawyer and the mother a philosophy professor. Before enrolling their child in a private school, the nine-year-old son was required to take a neuropsychiatric exam. The cost of this approximately eight-hour exam was $1,500 before insurance. The private day school in which they were enrolling their child cost $35,000 a year. In addition, the child was to have a summer tutor twice a week at $100 a session. How many children with dyslexia can have the best education that money can buy?

Today, many adults with dyslexia no longer feel stigmatized in sharing their struggles growing up with dyslexia and coping as successful adults. These individuals are terrific role models for younger dyslexics. However, young dyslexics whose parents do not value education, who do not understand dyslexia, and who accept unquestioningly what their superiors tell them, are at a distinct disadvantage. Some are too ill at ease to be assertive and unable to organize and keep records to participate in school conferences. Some, out of necessity, are too busy striving to provide the necessities of life even to show up at school and to see that homework comes home. Many do not have the mental and physical stamina to assist educationally at home. The parents who are unable to cry out for help are the ones who concern me the most.

According to Dr. Grover Whitehurst, former assistant secretary of education, U.S. Department of Education: "More American children suffer long-term harm from the process of learning to read than from parental abuse, accidents, and all other childhood diseases and disorders. In purely economic terms, reading-related difficulties cost our nation more than the war on terrorism, crime, and drugs combined."[55]

According to the International Dyslexia Association, current studies suggest that fifteen- to twenty-percent of the population has a learning disability. Of those, eighty-five percent have the specific learning disability known as dyslexia.

Kurita

These statistics triggered my memory and I began to contemplate Kurita, a first-grader in my class for one semester. I found three small packages wrapped in plain paper towels and fastened securely with gray duct tape after my class had gone home for the weekend. It was nearly Christmas, and I had the curiosity of a four year old. I tore a tiny opening in the towel of the smallest package: a used barrette.

An early Christmas gift?

I left the packages on my cluttered desk and locked up.

Monday arrived. Then Tuesday and finally, Wednesday, the long awaited day for our Christmas party that culminated with a two-week vacation. Recalling the paper-towel packages from last week, I placed them under our Christmas tree. After opening lovely gifts from several students, I reluctantly opened the mystery packages covered generously with wide gray tape: the barrette; a dirty, green glass mug; and a used writing slate with a pink wooden bear in the upper left corner. I showed my delight and gratitude, as I did with each student's gift. I was relieved that no one made a disparaging remark about the shabby wrappings or unusual contents.

Missing Identity

I could find no name or trace of the giver. Neither did any student volunteer a hint of identity. As I retreated deep into memory, I recalled that Kurita was present on Friday but had been absent the last three days. Could she have left her gifts on Friday? Kurita was a frail, petite student who struggled with first-grade reading. She was extremely shy, never initiating conversation and often speaking in phrases rather than complete sentences.

When showered with attention, she displayed the hint of a smile, dispelling the sadness which often overshadowed her charming face.

With the one clue, I played detective. From my students, I learned that Kurita was staying out of town with an uncle. My next checkpoint was the school office where tons of useful information was deposited, but rarely dispensed to those of us who had a right and need to know.

To my inquiry about Kurita's absence, the attendance clerk retorted, "Don't you read the newspaper?" I learned that over the weekend Kurita's father had stabbed her mother eight times, and Kurita had witnessed the brutal ordeal.

"Did she die?" I almost screamed at the clerk.

"Oh, the mother survived and is even home from the hospital," the clerk said.

Home Visit

Piercing screams, and blood spurting and spilling everywhere flashed through my mind. I could see Kurita recoiled in a dark corner as the tragedy took place. I collected cookie and candy treats from our party, along with a small gift I had for each student, and drove to Kurita's home. Going alone, I felt apprehensive about what I might find. Kurita's address led me to a large tan house in need of much repair. As I arrived, I spotted a handsome teenage boy playing catch ball with another boy in the street. I asked the boy in a hooded gray sweatshirt if I had the correct address.

He gave me a questioning look, paused, glanced at his playmate and said, "Yes, this is 1107 Madison Avenue."

With the address affirmed, I said, "I am Kurita's teacher from Blankenship School."

His aloofness turned to animation as his eyes met mine. Tossing the ball to his partner, he introduced himself as Quinten, Kurita's brother, and graciously invited me into the house.

Quinten apologized for the disarray as he escorted me through the dimly lit front room. He knocked at a partially opened door. Someone opened the door from the inside and I stood peering at a bedridden young woman surrounded by three or four adults and children. My eyes searched the room for Kurita while the quietly subdued audience stared at me with curiosity.

"This is Kurita's teacher," Quinten told the somber onlookers, and then he disappeared. The shushed children scurried out of the bedroom.

As I chatted briefly with Josey, the victim, I learned to my disappointment that Kurita was still with an uncle in the country.

"Did you know that Kurita's father almost killed me?"

"The school secretary told me you had been in the hospital." I was trying to avoid the words *father* and *kill.* As there were no available chairs, Josey invited me to sit on her bed.

"I am tough, though, and he is in jail. I am so sorry that Kurita heard her father come in drunk and saw him attack me. Quinten was spending the night with a friend." Josey spoke weakly, without moving in bed.

I listened and dug into the deep recesses of my mind to find words of comfort and encouragement. "You are surrounded by family and friends who care about you. You are an overcomer. Life will get better. Right now, concentrate on getting well."

Someone standing near the window said, "Josey, you need to stop thinking about that awful night and try to nap while your pain pill works."

I squeezed her hand as I said good-by. I left the bag of goodies and a note thanking Kurita for my gift. I pictured the timid grin on her face as she learned of my visit. As I turned to retrace my steps through the house, I noticed a darkened area that could have been dried blood beside a sofa. I thought I smelled blood, but maybe that came from Josey's bandaged wound. I left downcast because I did not get to hug Kurita and speak an affirming word.

In the meantime I placed one of Kurita's gifts, the green mug, in my dishwasher. The mug emerged sparkling clean, with a glistening golden rim. This love-filled mug remains in my curio cabinet as a prized possession and a reminder of a line from Robert Frost, "I have miles to go before I sleep."

Lost Opportunity

When school resumed after Christmas break, I learned that Kurita had moved and was attending another school. The opportunity was lost to shower her with love and attention to help bring her out of her shell and to help ease her trauma. No more opportunity to help this struggling reader as I never saw her again. Obviously, there were multiple problems. Did she learn to read? Is she one of the left-behind kids? As Dr. Whitehurst noted, did Kurita suffer more from reading failure than from parental abuse?

Chapter 28

Sandy

We make a living by what we get, but we make a life by what we give.

— Norman MacEwan

After retiring, I worked four years as a homebound teacher. I was assigned to Sandy while she was a seventh-grade student in 2001. To be placed on homebound, a physician had to sign that it was inadvisable for the student to attend school for medical or psychological reasons. A psychiatrist had signed Sandy's homebound permission paper.

A certified teacher could then see the student one hour twice a week at home or at a designated site. Homebound was meant to be temporary, and Sandy had a six-month respite from regular classes. The referring psychiatrist wrote on the homebound referral form: Can't concentrate, seems to be too restless. Diagnosis: Attention deficit hyperactive disorder. The psychiatrist's referral statement left me puzzled. Many in-school students would fit this category.

The school psychologist's most recent evaluation was done in 1999, and he recommended special education. While prior evaluations were not available to me, the current assessment reported: "Sandy is referred for an early re-evaluation due to her difficulties in the regular classroom in the areas of math and writing. She is making progress on her current IEP (individual education placement) goals in the area of reading comprehension."

What were the comprehension goals for this seventh-grader when the psychologist's report said she read the words *to, in,* and *dog* but was not successful reading the words *as, get, was, his,* and *when*? This report indicated that she was spending time in the regular classroom as well as special education. No mention was made of dyslexia in the report, but I began to suspect dyslexia in my first session with her.

As Sandy had been in homebound previously, my supervisor said, "You must find some place besides the home to work with Sandy. The home is lice-infested and filthy, with repugnant odors."

At my first meeting with Sandy, she was dressed in shorts and top, attire a bit cool for late fall. Her lifeless dark-brown hair flowed to the nape of her neck. I noticed her bold gray-green eyes as she pushed her hair from her face. She had a pretty face, her skin tanned from the sun; she would make a young man's heart flutter someday. She was cooperative and did not show signs of restlessness or inattention.

I examined the reading material her teacher had sent. "Sandy, would you read this sentence for me, please?" I asked and pointed to the sentence.

I quickly realized that the reading and language arts materials supplied by her special education teacher were totally beyond her achievement level. She could do the work only if I read everything to her. I administered the Gray Oral Reading Test and her achievement score was not even first grade level. She came with a seventh grade math book. While the first of the book was a review, Sandy could do the problems if I read directions and word problems to her.

Since I was with her only two hours a week much of the work was to be done at home. When I made assignments, Sandy returned with none of them. She simply could not read the material. I abandoned reading material sent by the special education teacher. I pulled out my *Merrill Linguistic Reader*—Book A, which deals with decodable short '*a*' words plus a few sight words. We started with such words as *cat, hat, can,* and *had*.

As we continued, Sandy's demeanor changed. She read with eagerness, even gusto, like a sponge soaking up water. However, the poor home conditions, friends from the wrong crowd, and years of trying and failing had affected Sandy's habits, self-concept, and aspirations. She started skipping appointments. Soon the family moved farther away from the library. We arranged for me to see Sandy at a public place closer to home. Her attendance continued to be poor; in fact, it was so sporadic I reported Sandy to my supervisor and her mother made a court appearance over truancy.

Finally, without telling my supervisor, I agreed to see Sandy at her home. I knew this was the only way to see her regularly. As I pulled into the unpaved driveway, I could see that half of a large windowpane was missing. As I sprayed lice insecticide on myself, I heard blaring music from across the street as three fellows huddled around a shiny black car.

Sandy's grandmother met me at the door. The grandmother was a plain woman who was very frustrated with Sandy and her mother's irresponsibility. I soon surmised that she was the most sensible member of the family.

I seated myself on a large footstool covered with navy, coarsely woven material, thinking there might be less of a chance of lice there than on the cluttered couch. In front of me was a door that led into the kitchen.

Through the doorway, I could see a low window with part of the pane missing. In this neighborhood, I wondered what kept thieves from invading while the grandmother, the mother, Sandy, and her sister slept.

To my right was another half-opened door to a room almost as dark as night. Litter was on the floor: books, toys, stale bread, and paper. Clothes were scattered on a chair, on the unmade bed, and on a windowsill beneath a dangling dark curtain.

No one else was home so the grandmother talked freely. "Trish (Sandy's mother) and her kids are draining me of the little pension I get. They have as much money as I do but they pester me until I give in. I am old and they get on my nerves until I can't take it anymore."

Then the grandmother shifted the conversation. "Thomas has been taken from us and put in a foster home."

Thomas was Sandy's brother. "When did this happen?" I asked.

"The social worker came for him last week after Trish's court hearing," the grandmother said as a tear dropped on her collar. "I am so afraid this is going to happen to Sandy and Bubbles, too." I assumed Bubbles was Sandy's younger sister.

Finally, Sandy appeared. Her grandmother chastised her for being late but Sandy offered no explanation. Soon after, Bubbles, whom I guessed to be about seven, came home and began begging the grandmother, unsuccessfully, for money. It was more difficult for Sandy to concentrate at home with the constant badgering of her little sister. Sandy and I completed our hour together and I made another appointment, being careful to write every detail to leave with the family.

I continued to see Sandy. Sometimes she would be home at our appointed time, sometimes she would come in late, and sometimes the grandmother could provide me with no information about her whereabouts. I often left without seeing Sandy.

Late one Friday afternoon, the music across the street was unusually loud and there was a gang of young people hanging around. I saw a police car drive slowly by the house—not a strange sight for that part of town.

The grandmother volunteered, "The police raided that house last weekend. Illegal drugs were being sold."

No surprise to me, I thought to myself.

Sandy, her mother, and Bubbles all tried to talk at once as each attempted to tell her version of the story. "It was after dark and we saw four police cars. We turned the lights out and lay low on the floor so we could see across the street," said Sandy, all worked up.

Bubbles said, "When those dudes came out, they had chains around their hands and legs."

"Were you afraid?" I inquired.

"Naw. When we were on Seventeenth Street, someone was shot next door. We didn't see him but we heard three shots and saw an ambulance," Sandy replied bravely.

Another time when I was waiting for Sandy, I thought I saw movement on the floor through the kitchen door. The first time I just dismissed the fleeting movement as imagination. The second time confirmed that I really did see the gray, swift movement of a small animal. Again, I rationalized that a stray cat had come through the broken window. However, on the third passage, I knew what I saw—a rat had been scurrying back and forth. I endured.

I am not sure how much I was able to do for Sandy academically. Would her life have been different if she had received help in kindergarten or first grade? Could this cycle of welfare-dependence have been broken? Could the road that leads to juvenile delinquency have been blocked?

Chapter 29
Struggles with Legislation

A dream doesn't become reality through magic; it takes determination and hard work.

—Colin Powell

The word *dyslexia* has been in federal legislation since the passage of Public Law 94-142, which Congress enacted in 1975.[56] The law states that a free appropriate public education would be available for all handicapped children no later than September 1, 1980. How many educators, much less parents, were made aware of PL 94-142 at that time or even know about it today?

Off and Running

In 2006, Mike Bruce, a board member of the Dyslexia Association of the Pennyrile, said to me, "Write something up and I will give it to my dad." At that time Mike's dad, Representative James Bruce, had served in the Kentucky Legislature longer than any other representative had, and he was highly revered by both Democrats and Republicans. Mike, like so many parents, recognized his own struggles with dyslexia, after a family member had been diagnosed.

I grabbed my copy of the Texas Dyslexia Law, which went into effect in 1987 as the first state law. The Texas law is still the most comprehensive state dyslexia law. I extracted a few key points, had other board members and educators read these ideas, and gave them to him. "Mike, if we can do nothing more than get dyslexia defined in state law, we will have been successful."

Parents *Can* Make a Difference

Sometime later, my phone rang. "Hello, I'm Jana Thompson and I have a son with dyslexia," a timid voice confided.

I thought to myself, *How many hundreds of times have I picked up my phone to a similar introduction?*

However, the conversation took a different turn. "I heard about your efforts to try to get a law passed to help dyslexic children. I want to help," Jana said.

I listened attentively as Jana painfully told me about her third-grade son, Jay. "My son was in public school and failing despite the fact that we spent at least two hours on homework each night. He is a highly intelligent but troubled child. He sometimes explodes in tears as any pressure infuriates him. Then I feel guilty and ashamed that I pressured him to that point."

"Tell me more about school," I said.

"His problems escalated in third grade. He tried very hard but those red marks on his papers crushed him. We would study spelling all week until I was sure he knew every word, but he would come home dejected, saying, 'Mom, I failed spelling again.' You know how cruel other students can be. They laughed at him when he tried to read aloud. The teacher thought he didn't study and became exasperated with him at first and then later, ignored him.

We had him tested and discovered the dyslexia. School officials said they had no one to teach dyslexics. Although we couldn't afford to do so, we scraped up the money to put him in Shedd Academy."[57]

Jana went on, "I've made many trips to Rep. Nesler's office, pleading for his help. Both he and his staff have listened to my despair and promised to help."

We were delighted to have this dauntless young mother join our cause. After all, our cause was for the Jays of the world. In a few days, members of our dyslexia board, parents, and I went to Frankfort, Kentucky, our capital. There were Jana and the director of Shedd Academy, Dr. Paul Thompson. Rep. Bruce had arranged a meeting with the chairperson of the Senate Education Committee, Sen. Ken Winters. We nearly filled the conference room. I think Sen. Winters was a bit surprised and flustered by our urgency. However, after many contacts with him in Frankfort and in his hometown of Murray, I regarded him as a politician who was willing to listen.

On that visit to the Legislature, I also witnessed Rep. Nesler take Jana *under his wing* and introduce her to persons who could make things happen. Nesler introduced HB 680, proposing that "dyslexia be recognized as a specific learning disability requiring specialized instruction."[58]

— *Paducah Sun*, March 2, 2006.

Later, I picked up my phone to hear Rep. Bruce's excited voice. "Our bill passed the House 92-0. We are on our way to becoming one of the first states in the nation with a dyslexia law."

The next phone call, however, was bad news. The Senate did not concur with the House, saying, "Dyslexia is in the administrative regulations; therefore, Kentucky does not need a law."

Soon after, Jana's husband received a transfer to Alaska. Our rock-solid proponent, whose emotional appeal had the potential to penetrate the lofty facade of the most ardent opponent in the House, was gone.

The next year we had a first-term representative, James Carr, who understood dyslexia and related disabilities. Rep. Carr tried to push dyslexia legislation but was told by the then-chairperson of the House Education Committee that "Dyslexia is just a passing fantasy." He compared dyslexia to a new flavor of ice cream.

Representative Tilley

The Dyslexia Association of the Pennyrile was undaunted. In 2008, Rep. Bruce retired after forty-two years in the House. Elected to replace Bruce was John Tilley, a smart, energetic attorney.

Determined, we immediately began talking dyslexia. The Kentucky Legislature is only in session a few months each year, beginning in January. A dyslexia bill needed to be filed prior to the start of the legislative session in order to wind its way through the process, especially if we encountered roadblocks. Therefore, we started our barrage during the summer. I rang Rep. Tilley's phone, left documents at his office, sent e-mails, and prodded him at church until he finally became exasperated and told me to *bug off*. He told me he had to spend some time with his family. I understood and respected his wishes.

When fall arrived, I started badgering him again. However, despite my persistence, I could not get him to move fast enough. Michael Kaczor, a professional advocate from New Mexico, was working with a client in our area. He convinced the Dyslexia Association of the Pennyrile that he could help get the dyslexia bill passed. John Hopson, president of our board, and I agreed to help pay Michael's fee and expenses.

Like dry soil absorbs water, Michael soaks in information regarding regulations and how to work with school systems to the advantage of parents. He was of unwavering help to us, and we were able to garner like-minded people from all over Kentucky. The movement was no longer just a western Kentucky issue.

Speed Demon

Realizing that we needed support from the State Department of Education for a dyslexia bill to be successful, I was amazed when I was able to get an appointment with the then-Commissioner of Education, Jon Draud. *Wow, I have an appointment with the top education official in the state.* Michael happened to be working with a client in western Kentucky and could go with me.

I also invited two parents from Lexington, who were distressed over the lack of support their dyslexic children were getting. The drive from my home to Frankfort is slightly over two-hundred miles; and I had to drive about forty-five minutes in the opposite direction to pick up Michael at Barkley Lodge.

Of all days, my alarm clock chose that day to malfunction. I awoke quite late. I jumped into my clothes, ran a comb through my hair, did a few strokes with a toothbrush, grabbed a chocolate-chip granola bar and oh, I just *had* to take two minutes to make a cup of coffee.

I took off in the dark, maneuvering the curves and hills and jumping with the bumps in the road. The highway was almost totally mine at 4:30 that morning. I found Michael in a stew, pacing back and forth in the parking area of Barkley Lodge.

"Michael, sorry I am so late. I had a problem," I was too humiliated to explain further.

Michael did not say much but looked irritated as he checked his watch. He almost fell into the front seat and slammed the car door with startling force.

I hit the gas pedal and was soon on the Western Kentucky Parkway. Shortly, a blinding sun began to cloud my vision. Michael searched for my sunshades, but I concluded I had left them at home. My eyes stayed glued to the road, though, as I drove, unmindful of the speed limit. Michael watched for connecting roads. As we neared Frankfort, I realized needed gas. I pulled into a service station long past its prime. I ran to the bathroom while Michael filled my car with gas and even forged my signature on my credit-card receipt. Fastest gas fill-up in history.

As I got back on the Bluegrass Parkway, I accelerated to nearly ninety miles an hour, unmindful of the possibility of a speeding ticket. We were going to be late for our 9:00 a.m. appointment with the chief educator in Kentucky. Michael tried to console me as he twisted in his seat and swallowed hard. I guess he feared for his life.

We arrived safely, fifteen minutes late for our appointment. The secretary ushered us in. I felt dizzy and depleted as Comm. Draud, Dr. Larry Taylor,

Director of Special Education, and his assistant stared at us. Our two parents were there at the appointed time and took advantage of the opportunity to tell their stories. After fifteen minutes, Comm. Draud excused himself, but Dr. Taylor was generous with his time. Still reeling from the whirlwind drive, I let Michael do most of the talking. Unlike so many persons in positions of authority who talk without pause to keep from listening to others, Dr. Taylor listened intently as we pleaded our case for students with dyslexia.

Before Michael returned to New Mexico, I tried appeasing him with a small bottle of Jack Daniel's. I prayed that my minister would not see me going into the liquor store.

My One Stint at Stalking

Being a perfectionist and wanting to make sure that the legislation was moving forward, I contacted Rep. Tilley, who was the bill's sponsor, in 2009. Legislators are busy people, and Rep. Tilley was no exception, but I was determined. Sometimes his colleague, Rep. Myron Dossett, also a strong supporter of the bill, would pass messages back and forth.

Rep. Tilley finally forced me into being more creative—or was it stalking?

I knew that our local legislators recorded a radio and TV report on Saturdays when they came home.

Here was my chance to meet them face-to-face. How could I find this taping?

I intently listened to a radio announcer who mentioned having an appointment for taping an update with our legislators. Where would that taping take place? What time would this occur? I thought of the community college, which had a nice studio. *I'll drive out to the college to see if I can find any vehicles with radio- or TV-station call letters on them. Another clue would be the special license plate legislators have on their cars*, I said to myself.

Bingo. As I turned into the long driveway of the community college, I spotted a car with the call letters WKDZ. Driving farther, I spotted a car with a legislative plate. Which building are these people in? I vaguely remembered where the recording studio was. I simply took a seat on the floor outside the closed door and waited for Rep. Tilley's exit. From then on, when I needed a brief session with our legislators, I found them. Sometimes that conference occurred as I walked with Tilley to his car.

Candy and Jokes

In early 2009, John Hopson, our dyslexia association president, and I made a trip to Frankfort and persuaded Rep. Carl Rollin, chairperson of the House Education Committee, to place the dyslexia bill on the agenda of the next meeting of the House

Education Committee. John carried a basket of candy that sweetened the secretaries, and he entertained them with his jokes. While John was doing this, I roamed the halls and offices discussing our bill. As I met people dressed in black suits, white shirts, and ties, I would start a conversation by saying, "You must be someone really important around here." Usually, the person would reply, "I am Rep. _____." With that introduction, I started talking about our bill.

Down to Business

On Monday night, after our appointment with Rep. Rollin, twenty or so of us gathered at a hotel to discuss our strategy for the House Education Committee meeting the next morning. Rep. Addia Wuchner, from the northern part of the state and our own Myron Dossett joined us. In addition to being a highly respected, articulate representative, Wuchner also has a dyslexic son and grandson who have not been supported by the educational system.

At eight the next morning, our clan members seated themselves behind the testifying area facing the legislators. Rep. Tilley, who had been away for two days due to a family illness, breezed in and escorted me into the hall. "I didn't know we were on the House Education Committee agenda until yesterday. I asked that we be last on the agenda. We are not organized," he said.

From meeting the previous evening, I was able to discern the more knowledgeable and articulate in our group. I introduced Lois Weinberg from the Hindman Settlement School, Hindman, Kentucky, to Rep. Tilley and went back to my seat. This school has had a program for dyslexic persons, using a method similar to ours, since the early 1980s.

Rep. Tilly quickly took command and calmly orchestrated the hearing before the House education committee. He called on Lois to give her testimony. She was at ease as she answered questions from the inquisitive committee members, responding with passion and depth of knowledge. I sat in awe at the representatives' level of understanding of the need for legislation. They were engaged and seemed determined that something could and must be done for persons with dyslexia.

One representative spoke up, "I knew Dr. Shedd back in the 1970s and operated a tutoring program out of my garage using his method. I think this bill should be called the Shedd Dyslexia Bill."

Several committee members elevated Rep. Tilley to hero status for bringing the plight of persons with dyslexia to the attention of the House. The dyslexia bill passed with only one opposing vote.

Surprisingly, our greatest opposition came from educators themselves. In my opinion, their opposition came from not understanding dyslexia and from fear that more work would be piled on their already overloaded schedules.

In the hallway after the education committee meeting, I was ecstatic. I was astonished, after having met with so much resistance, that the House was so receptive. In fact, I told my friends, "If this bill passes and is signed by the governor, it will be one of the happiest days of my life." We were on a roll.

Wrong again. Since there was the proverbial funding issue, the bill went to the Ways and Means Committee. The joke in Frankfort is that the Ways and Means Committee is the "graveyard committee." If the leadership does not want a bill to pass, it is sent to Ways and Means to die. I personally went to the chairperson of the Ways and Means Committee and begged him to put our bill on his committee's agenda. He had bigger fish to fry, and the legislative session was soon over with our bill dead and buried.

In 2010 a dyslexia bill made it to the Senate where some senator attached a charter-schools amendment onto our bill. In the waning days of the legislature, charter schools had become an issue because Kentucky had lost its bid for a big chunk of money over not having charter schools. The deadline for filing new bills had long passed and the charter-school proponent's only chance was to attach an amendment on a bill headed for passage. With the amendment, our bill had to go back to committee. The Senate approved the dyslexia bill with the amendment on the last day of the

2010 session. Even though the House worked until nearly midnight, time ran out before representatives could act.

Absurd as it is, the same dilemma arose in 2011. Starting in the House and easily making its way to the Senate, our dyslexia bill had another unrelated amendment attached to it. The amendment had nothing to do with dyslexia. Again, the problem was timing. The legislative session was over before affirmative action was taken.

As I conclude this chapter in 2012, I exultantly report that HB 69, our dyslexia bill, passed both houses of the General Assembly, and Governor Steve Beshear has signed it. Jane Bruce, the mother of Mike Bruce (who played a vital role in planting the seeds of our dyslexia bill) and I were present at the governor's ceremonial signing. Many Kentuckians played a role in seeing this bill to fruition. In my mind, I saw thousands of little faces changing from frowns to smiles and teachers headed to their classrooms with the confidence that their students' struggles had lessened. Just as a firefighter cannot describe the elation and relief of pulling a child from a burning house, I have no words to describe my feelings.

Rep. Wuchner and Rep. Linda Belcher, whom Rep. Tilley had asked to take charge of a dyslexia bill after our defeat in 2009, were among those present. These two representatives were persistent and unyielding, as they understood the anguish of persons with dyslexia.

What made the difference in 2012? Certainly persistence played a role. Maybe we just learned how to play the game of politics. Legislative friends told us as we began that it often takes five years to get a bill through the Legislature.

In the last few years, states have been passing legislation so rapidly that I have lost count of the number of states with dyslexia laws. There are at least twelve.

Now that we have a dyslexia law, is that going to ensure student identification and appropriate remediation? Of course not, but it was an enormously important step worth fighting for. As Joyce Pickering, Director Emerita of the Shelton School in Dallas, Texas, told me in private conversation, "We can legislate, but we have to educate."

Chapter 30

Cost of Dyslexia

For of all sad words of tongue or pen, the saddest are these: It might have been.
— John Greenleaf Whittier

Throughout this book, I have written about the pain of dyslexia among persons I have known and with whom I have worked—and their families.

The inability to read can be a life-or-death issue. Recently, I read of the suicide of Joey Ferrara, a thirteen-year-old struggling student from California who had been diagnosed with severe dyslexia. [59]

Attending the International Dyslexia Conference a few years ago, Geraldine Miller, the leader behind the twenty-plus- year-old dyslexia bill in Texas, spoke about her only child, a dyslexic, taking his life. Mrs. Miller served as chairperson of the state Board of Education for a number of years and fought to see that Texas was the first state in the nation to have a dyslexia law.

Statistics tell the story. One study done in Los Angeles found that fifty percent of students committing suicide had been diagnosed with some type of learning disability. A teen with a learning disability such as dyslexia is ten times more likely to commit suicide as someone without a learning difficulty. A study in Canada examined the suicide notes left by two-hundred sixty-seven teens. Eighty-nine percent of the notes had spelling and grammatical errors indicative of learning disabilities.[60]

Unfortunately, we have had similar tragedies happen in our own area.

Imagine signing a form agreeing to a hysterectomy that you did not choose. Think of the danger involved in not being able to read street signs. How would it feel to go into a voting booth unable to vote for your chosen candidate? What would happen if a non-reader incorrectly read the prescription label on his child's medicine bottle?

In addition, there is the financial cost of dyslexia. Money talks to legislators. As I began this chapter, I was hoping to find enough research to approximate the cost per-year of dyslexia in dollars and cents to our nation. I wanted a graph that would give the cost of un-remediated dyslexia. I found putting the cost in a neat package impossible. First, much of the financial research is old. Second, costs vary from state to state and data is not available for all states. Third, it is impossible to determine the dropout rate. Dyslexia is never written into school records as the reason a student dropped out of high school.

Furthermore, as we look at the cost in dollars and cents, terms that have slightly different meanings are used. The terms *dyslexia*, *learning disability*, and *specific learning disability* are often used interchangeably. They need clarification.

We would expect, in any control group, to find a greater number with a learning disability, slightly fewer with a specific-learning disability, and about fifteen percent less with dyslexia. Which term is used and what that term means to the researcher can make a difference. I found it impossible to do more than approximate the cost of dyslexia.

I hope these terms will help the reader muddle through the figures in this chapter and understand why an accurate monetary calculation is impossible.

Learning disability—"A disorder that results in learning challenges that are not caused by low intelligence, problems with hearing or vision, or lack of educational opportunity. Many children with learning disabilities have difficulties in particular skill areas, such as reading or language skills. These children may also have difficulties with paying attention..."[61]

Learning disability is a more general term. The National Council of Learning Disabilities lists twenty-four million persons with learning disabilities.

About a year ago, I had the opportunity to attend a magic-therapy workshop done by a leading authority on the therapeutic use of magic. This person, brilliant and highly educated, works with mental-health professionals and teachers around the world. In giving an example of his work, he referred to a group of children with learning disabilities. He spotted one boy who used exceptionally keen thinking in analyzing the logic behind the magic. Reportedly, he asked the teacher why this very bright boy was in a class of students with learning disabilities. Obviously, *learning disability* to him meant "slow to learn." *Learning disability* to him did not include persons with dyslexia, often average or above in intelligence. Just look at the long list of great dyslexic achievers in business, the arts, entertainment, sports, politics, and science. Think of Harrison Ford, Stephen J. Cannell, Bruce Jenner, Tommy Hilfiger, Magic Johnson, and Robin Williams. This is an example of how the umbrella term *learning disability* is misunderstood.

Specific learning disability—"An impairment of learning ability that may affect one or more academic areas, but not others, and that exists in spite of adequate intelligence and opportunity to learn."[62] For example, a person may be good in math or mechanical problem solving but poor in reading. *Specific learning disability* does not include intellectual abilities that create limitations in mental functioning.

Dyslexia, according to the National Council of Learning Disabilities, is defined as "difficulty in reading, spelling, writing, and related language skills that results from an impairment in the way the brain processes information." [63]

Dyslexia (reading), dyscalculia (math), and dysgraphia (writing) are considered specific learning disabilities.

Reading problems can be due to many factors such as irregular school attendance, poor home conditions, inadequate teaching—and would fall under literacy issues.

In an astonishing article from the *Washington Post*, Jay Mathews refers to a survey released by the National Center for Learning Disabilities in which two-thousand Americans shared beliefs about learning disabilities. Forty-three percent believe that learning disabilities correlate with IQ. This idea may have originated from the fact that students with learning disabilities were once placed in special education classes with low IQ students.

Mr. Mathews goes on to say that fifty-five percent believe that corrective eyewear can treat certain learning disabilities, and twenty-two percent think that learning disabilities can be caused by spending too much time watching the computer or television. Other causes on the list are poor diet, childhood vaccinations, poor parenting, or poor teaching in early childhood.[64] I would like to see other surveys to check out this degree of ignorance. Because the terms defined in this chapter are used interchangeably, maybe I should not be surprised.

I recently spoke to a church group about dyslexia. A retired army colonel with two master's degrees said afterwards, "I didn't know what dyslexia was." In the forty-two years the Dyslexia Association of the Pennyrile has existed in this area, the media have been extremely generous with their coverage of dyslexia. My guess is that hundreds of announcements, feature stories, ads, and interviews have taken place. I was aghast at his lack of knowledge and wondered how many more citizens were not reached. I can only conclude that the public often ignores dyslexia until a relative or close friend has problems.

On the other hand, Mr. Matthews' article has good news about dyslexia. Ninety-percent know that dyslexia is a learning disability. He also says eighty-percent can define dyslexia but he does not share what the participants' definitions are. [65]

Poverty

Harry Sylvester in *Legacy of the Blue Heron* says, "Studies have found that over half of the people who are receiving public assistance have learning disabilities. " [66] According to the National Institute of Child Health and Human Development, approximately eighty-five percent of all individuals with learning disabilities have difficulties in reading. Forty-eight percent of those with learning disabilities are out of the workforce or unemployed.[67] According to the National Institute for Literacy, only five-percent of Americans with strong literacy skills live in poverty. On the other hand, seventy-five percent of unemployed adults have reading or writing difficulties.[68] (Figures arrived at before the 2008 plus recession.) Literacy Partners, Inc. says that low literacy skills cost the nation nearly two-hundred billion dollars a year. [69]

Juvenile and Prison Population

According to the U. S. Department of Education, sixty-percent of America's prison inmates are illiterate and eighty-five percent of all juvenile offenders have reading problems."[70] Dr. Kathryn Currier Moody in *Dyslexia in the Prison Population* says the American prison population has topped two million inmates. "[71] It costs about thirty-five thousand dollars per year to keep an individual in prison," she reports. Her study was conducted at the University of Texas Medical Branch with the Texas Department of Criminal Justice in 2000; the cost for Texas may be even higher today.

Other states such as Kentucky report a cost of nineteen-thousand per year for one inmate.[72] In Dr. Currier's research, the incidence of dyslexia among the prison population was forty-eight percent, twice the prevalence in the general population.

Timothy

As a part-time reading instructor at a community college, I worked with a former prison inmate. This was a burly, muscular man in his thirties but looked more like forty. His bushy eyebrows with dark eyes underneath often avoided mine. Even in winter, his skin looked tanned. Years behind bars, I surmised, hardened his facial expression. He was punctual in attendance, gave informed answers in class, but could not read simple words. I suspected dyslexia after a couple of classes but waited to build rapport before confronting him with that possibility.

Early in the semester he blurted out, "I am an ex-con." I did not ask and he never divulged the nature of his crime or the length of his imprisonment. He did tell me that he had earned his GED at this college. "I had to take the history test seven times before I passed it. I will not give up," he said with determination.

I could not believe any student would require that many tries. Most students would have given up after two or three attempts. I went to the director of Adult Education, and yes, he did make seven attempts before he finally passed that part of the GED. He had a very low reading level but knew the content. He did not know that he could have the test read to him. I felt ashamed at questioning the truth of what he told me just because he called himself an ex-con.

When I did discuss his reading difficulty, he was not at all familiar with dyslexia but readily acknowledged his reading problem. He also told me he had been turned away from job opportunities because he had been in prison. He took my suggestion and sought screening for dyslexia through the Dyslexia Association of the Pennyrile with one of our scholarships. His dyslexia was confirmed.

Then Timothy asked the all-important question, "What do I do about my dyslexia?"

I did not have an answer. I discussed our community dyslexia program with him. He sometimes had night classes and he did not have the gas money for an extra trip to our area. Timothy lived with his parents and needed a job now. The Adult Education Department could not remediate a severely dyslexic person. The goal of my class was to help improve students' skills so they would be successful with college courses. Timothy was working toward a certificate in a technical program such as welding, electricity, car repair. Of course, some reading is required in these jobs.

I recall giving a vocabulary test. Timothy struggled and was the last student to finish. I glimpsed his crestfallen face and heard him sigh as he left the room. He did very poorly on the test—so poorly that I was afraid he would be devastated when I returned the test paper. I was worried that he might drop out of the class. His reaction was just the opposite. Yes, he expressed disappointment with his score but he said, "I will never, never, never give up." I made sure he passed my class.

If Timothy had been matched with a one-to-one tutor trained to teach persons with severe dyslexia, things might have turned out differently for him. How might his life have been different if his dyslexia was diagnosed in the primary grades and remediation begun then?

Education

In my teaching career, I have met students with dyslexia who often repeated a grade or two. What else did we know to do with them? The National Association of School Psychologists estimates that grade-repeating costs well over fourteen-billion dollars a year. Retention affects about 2.4 million people. Twenty-seven percent of children with learning disabilities drop out of high school, according to the twenty-third annual Report to Congress by the U. S. Department of Education (2001). [73]

Cost is not the only factor to consider. What about the negative effects on self-esteem?

Other sources estimate that as many as thirty-five percent of children diagnosed with a learning disability drop out of high school. According to figures supplied by the International Dyslexia Association, thirty-one percent of students with a learning disability who drop out are arrested within three-to-five years of leaving school. Furthermore, the International Dyslexia Association lists sixty percent of substance abusers with a learning disability.

Remember: many of these children are highly intelligent and creative. What a waste of human potential.

PART FOUR

CHANGES

Chapter 31

Looking Backward—Focusing Forward

I don't know what your destiny will be, but one thing I know: the only ones among you who will be really happy are those who will have sought and found how to serve.

—Albert Schweitzer

A s I searched for an appropriate closing for this book, I thought of Robert Frost's poem, *The Road Not Taken*:

> *Two roads diverged in a wood, and I*
> *I took the one less traveled by,*
> *and that has made all the difference.*

While references to dyslexia are found dating back to the late 1800s, I think of Dr. Samuel T. Orton as standing where the two roads diverged. He took the road less traveled, which set us on the correct path to understanding and helping persons with dyslexia. He met many people along the way such as June Lyday

Orton, Anna Gillingham, and Bessie Stillman. He did not tread that path alone.

We have miles to go but our pace is vastly increasing. The world for a person with dyslexia is not changing fast enough—not for the eleven-year-old child who burns his hand because he cannot read the sign that says *hot, do not touch,* or the door sign *private* and enters a room only to be scolded for barging in on an important meeting. We are on a bumpy but paved road today, not a path. In fact, as I complete the final chapter in this book, I am still updating newly released information. Here are some areas where debris, potholes, and mudslides remain obstructions as we diligently work to overcome these hurdles.

School personnel, parents, and the public are beginning to accept dyslexia as a real entity. Recently, I read the evaluation report, done by a local school psychologist, who actually used the word *dyslexia.* With the research being done on the brain by Drs. Bennet Shaywitz and Sally Shaywitz at the National Institute of Child Health and Human Development, Yale Center, and many others, and with the use of fMRIs, we are able to see differences in the brains of dyslexics versus non-dyslexics. Dyslexia is no longer an illusion.

The American Psychiatric Association has been working on revising its *Diagnostic and Statistical Manual.* The association collected suggestions from both the public and professionals for at least a year. APA held conferences to wade through the issues on particular topics. The manual was written and field-tested, revised, and tested again. Early on, APA proposed the word *dyslexia*. I could not wait to inform some of my professional friends who are "doubting Thomases" that dyslexia was going to be in their diagnostic bible.

Earlier this year, I mentioned dyslexia to a retired local physician who has had a successful career in our community. His reaction was "What is dyslexia?" He went on to explain that no agreed-upon criteria have been established for a diagnosis of dyslexia. I held his attention long enough to mention that the *American Psychiatric Association's Diagnostic and Statistical Manual* is slated to use the term *dyslexia* in its revised manual to be released in 2013. His denial of dyslexia shifted as he said, "Oh, then, criteria that define dyslexia will be established."

Horror struck me when I checked APA's website, May 2, 2012. APA had taken out *dyslexia* along with the diagnostic criteria that defined it. Instead APA had included every minute disorder (some I had never heard of), but the disorder we think of as dyslexia was a hodgepodge of confusion. I fired off an e-mail to APA so fast that the recipient probably thought I was illiterate, if anyone read my e-mail at all. Then I phoned, but I was unable to learn anything.

After researching phone numbers and e-mail addresses for a number of important people, I started contacting individuals such as the executive director at IDA, Joyce Pickering, Susan Barton, Sally Shaywitz, Maryann Wolf, and others of great influence. Those persons I contacted did not know of APA's latest change. Apparently, APA made the website change the day before my discovery. Individuals and organizations had only six weeks for a final response. I prided myself on starting the contacts as early as possible.

As I followed responses, I was extremely pleased with national efforts. I applaud The International Dyslexia Association, both the Executive Board and their Scientific Advisory Board, for its strong position on the issue and efforts to inform and involve the membership. In the position paper issued by the International Dyslexia Association, May 29, 2012, the association makes a strong plea for the reinstatement of dyslexia and gives clear rationale. The full text is on the Association's website: www. interdys. org.

IDA's president, Eric Tidas, MD, developmental and behavioral pediatrician and director of the Tridas Center for Child Development in Tampa, Florida, strongly supports IDA's official statement. He says, "It is imperative that the term 'dyslexia' be used in order for students and families to access assessment, effective treatment and support services."

Susan Barton sent e-mails to a vast number of contacts. I just hope those thousands of persons directly affected by dyslexia were aware of what APA was attempting and realized the important of their calls, e-mails, and letters.

We wait for the American Psychiatric Association's reaction to the pressure from organizations and individuals. If you were one of those desperate parents advocating for appropriate help for your child and learned of this impending setback, I hope the American Psychiatric Association heard your voice. Progress will come only as we unite with uncompromising persistence and speak loudly and clearly. We cannot leave the yearning for progress to only those professionals in lofty positions. We all can do something.

In my opinion, we have an inconsistency between the definition of dyslexia in federal law and national and international organizations. The federal regulations state: "Children with specific learning disabilities exhibit a disorder in one or more of the basic psychological processes involved in understanding or using spoken or written language... These include conditions that have been referred to as dyslexia."

There is something wrong with that definition. The National Center for Learning Disabilities classified dyslexia as a neurological disorder. The Learning Disability Association uses the term *learning disability* instead of *dyslexia* but refers to neurologically based learning disabilities.

Persons with dyslexia can have psychological problems, but these are separate from dyslexia.

Dyslexia is not a psychological disorder but a neurological disorder. Neurology has to do with the brain and nervous system. In the research laboratories where differences are clearly visible between the dyslexic and non-dyslexic brain, aren't we seeing a neurological difference?

Likewise, I must question the Individuals with Disabilities Education Act (IDEA, 2004) and Federal Code (300. 7), which both use outdated terms or undefined terms, in my opinion.

Brain injury and dyslexia are two entirely different entities, according to current thinking in my circle of comrades. Neither am I sure what *minimal brain dysfunction* is. Could this be archaic term leftover from the 1960s and 1970s? In those days the cause of dyslexia was associated with conditions such as oxygen deprivation during or after birth and certain illnesses while the mother was carrying the baby.

Climbing another hill on our road began in May 2012. Reps. Pete Stark (D-Calif) and Bill Cassidy (R-La), along with Dr. Shaywitz and others, established the Congressional Dyslexia Caucus.[74] One of Dr. Shaywitz's concerns has been the lack of accommodations afforded students with dyslexia in entrance exams for higher education.

For example, a brilliant student with dyslexia with an outstanding achievement record cannot get into medical school because he cannot pass the entrance exams. If the student were given additional time in taking the exam, he could pass and enter the world of his dreams, becoming a scientist to advance research in medicine or a diplomat capable of settling disputes among nations.

Testing accommodations are required under the Americans with Disabilities Act. However, Reps. Stark and Cassidy go on to say:

> *Many testing companies routinely ignore diagnoses of dyslexia and refuse to offer accommodations. We have heard numerous examples of bright, hardworking dyslexic young men and women who, with accommodations, have succeeded in school only to be stopped in their tracks because they are refused accommodations on tests. This has to stop.*[75]

I am encouraged by the organizational model known as Response-to-Intervention or RTI. RTI is a three-tier approach to early intervention. RTI usually begins with the screening of all children in the general-education classroom. Students identified with the possibility of learning issues are provided with reading intervention by general-education teachers, special educators, and reading specialists.

Progress is closely monitored. Students not progressing at *Tier 1* are moved to *Tier 2* for more intense instruction. If sufficient progress is not made in *Tier 2*, students are moved to *Tier 3*. At any time in the progression, a parent can request a full psychological evaluation. RTI only goes through the third grade. However, this organization is appropriate for any grade level. In my opinion, one of the strong points of RTI is the prevention of failure.

Although RTI has been extensively researched by some of the most credentialed persons in the field of dyslexia, I urge caution. First, this approach must be organized and supervised consistent with research data. Teachers must have training, especially as students are moved into Tiers 2 and 3. If students are moved through the tiers without adequate progress through third grade, crucial teaching time has been lost. Unless used properly, RTI can become a wait-to-fail program.

I strongly encourage abandoning the *discrepancy model* alluded to elsewhere in this book. Through the discrepancy model, a learning disability or dyslexia is determined primarily through a combination of intellectual- and achievement-testing. There must be a certain number of points between intelligence and achievement. That number of points is arbitrary and can vary from state to state.

The discrepancy formula fails to take into consideration our inability to measure intelligence with complete accuracy. Some students will be included who don't really need to be. More likely, as was the case with young students whom I taught, the discrepancy formula will exclude students who have dyslexia.

At one point in the process of revising its *Diagnostic and Statistical Manual,* the American Psychiatric Association proposed the elimination of the discrepancy formula. We await their recommendation. At present, federal law allows states to decide whether to use the discrepancy formula.

On May 2, 2012, the International Dyslexia Association released a list of nine university programs in the U. S. that have met the standards outlined in *IDA Knowledge and Practice Standards for Teachers of Reading.* The release states that IDA plans to offer certification based on these standards in the future. This step involves certifying university programs, whereas IMSLEC's mission was to offer endorsement of individual teachers/tutors. Getting courses in colleges so teachers are taught to make direct application of diagnostic and teaching methodology is crucial. Appendix A contains a list of these nine universities.

In 2009 Texas passed HB 461, [76] which outlines the nation's first legislation granting licensure for dyslexia practitioners and dyslexia therapists. College course requirements are explicitly detailed. For the dyslexia therapist, two-hundred hours of course work and seven-hundred hours of supervised clinical experience in multisensory education are required.

A competency exam is also required. Education officials hope this legislation will encourage teachers to seek licensure either at the practitioner or therapist level. I hope that Texas' efforts will serve as a model for a dyslexia program of studies in other teacher colleges.

On the other hand, I see a tendency on the part of some individuals to lump all reading problems under *literacy*. Such diffusion could become a huge setback along the road. Persons with dyslexia require a specific type of remediation.

Looking Back

If I look back to my beginnings, I hear a professor at George Peabody College, one of the top teacher-training institutions in the world then and today, say to me, "Come. I don't know anything about dyslexia but we can learn together." Today, Peabody's professors are leaders in the field. In those days I would go to the Peabody library and read everything I could find on dyslexia. There wasn't much to read. Today, I can only read a small fraction of the material that comes into my home daily.

The crucial question is: "What are we doing with this new knowledge?"

Some people feel money is the issue. Throwing more money at this problem and doing the same thing we have been doing is not the solution. Yes, we need more money, but we must make changes so that money will bring results.

I recently met a teacher from an adjoining state. She introduced herself as a newly hired reading interventionist, but she added, "I know nothing about teaching reading."

When a colleague tells me, "Advocating for a child with dyslexia or suspected dyslexia can be tantamount to moving a cruise ship with a piece of string and your teeth," I wonder if we are lost on a detour. When my highly intelligent and motivated primary student tells me," My friends say I am dumb because I can't read," I shudder. We have taken the correct fork in the road, but let's pick up the pace to get the *dys* out of dyslexia.

Epilogue

Due to delays in the publication of this book, I am compelled to bring the reader up to date following the release of the *American Psychiatric Association Diagnostic Manual* in May 2013. Anticipation of this manual was discussed in chapters 27 and 32. Unfortunately, the *Manual* does not include the word, *dyslexia*. Instead, the term *specific learning disability* is used.

A psychologist can choose from the following categories: 315.00 with impairment in reading, 315.2 with impairment in written expression, and/or 315.1 with impairment in mathematics. The examiner also has the option of designating these categories as mild, moderate, or severe.

In my opinion, this is a major setback for persons with dyslexia.

Appendix A

University programs recognized by the International Dyslexia Association standards as aligned with IDA's knowledge and practice standards, 2012.

College of Mount Saint Joseph (Cincinnati, Ohio)
> Reading Endorsement
> Master of Arts in Reading Science

Colorado College (Denver, Colorado)
> Master of Arts in Teaching: Literacy
> Intervention Specialist Program

Fairleigh Dickinson (Teaneck, New Jersey)
> Orton Gillingham Teacher Certificate

Massachusetts General (Boston, Massachusetts)
> Certificate of Advanced Studies in Reading
> Master of Science in Speech-Language
> Pathology: Reading Concentration

Saint Joseph's (Philadelphia, Pennsylvania)
> Master of Science in Special Education

Simmons College (Boston, Massachusetts)

Master of Science in Special Education:
Language and Literacy

Southeastern University (Lakeland, Florida)
Bachelor of Science in Elementary Education
with Reading and ESOL Endorsements
Bachelor of Science/Master of Education in
Exceptional Student Education with Reading
and ESOL Endorsements

Southern Methodist University (Dallas, Texas)
Master of Education in Reading and Writing

University of Colorado (Colorado Springs)
Bachelor of Arts in Special Education
Master of Arts in Special Education
Dyslexia Specialist Certificate

Tennessee Center for the Study and Treatment of
Dyslexia
Graduate Certificate in Dyslexic Studies

Appendix B

Books on Dyslexia

Most books listed are general rather than technical. Some are old but timely. Most are available from Amazon.com or from the International Dyslexia Association, www.interdys.org.

Brock, L. Eide, M.D., and Fernette F. Eide, M.D. *The Dyslexic Advantage, Unlocking the Hidden Potential of the Dyslexic Brain.* New York: Penguin Group, 2011.

Clarke, Louise. *Can't Read, Can't Write, Can't Talk Too Good Either.* New York: Penguin Books, 1973.

Corcoran, John, with Carole C. Carlson. *The Teacher Who Couldn't Read.* Northern Ireland: Brehon Publishing Company, 1937, Dec. 5.

Critchley, Macdonald. *Developmental Dyslexia.* Springfield, Illinois: Charles C. Thomas Publisher, 1964, reprinted 1966. One of the first books I read on dyslexia. It is interesting to compare the thinking in 1964 with our knowledge today.

Duane, Drake D. editor, *Reading and Attention Disorders, Neurobiological Correlates*, New York: York Press, 1999.

Eckel, Wendy Sand. *Educating Tigers.* Baltimore: AmErica House, 2000.

Haan, Cinthia Coletti. *Literacy Policy, Ground-Breaking Blueprint for State Legislation.* San Francisco, CA: The Haan Foundation for Children in collaboration with the Government Affairs Committee, 1999.

Haan, Cinthia Coletti. *The Power to Act, Transforming Literacy and Education.* Cinthia Coletti, 2011.

Henry, Marcia K. Ph.D. and Susan Brickley. *Dyslexia … Samuel T. Orton and His Legacy.* New York: International Dyslexia Association, July 1999.

High Noon Books (www.HighNoonBooks.com) has a series of controlled-vocabulary, easy-to-read books for the beginning reader.

Hubbell V, *Harvey. Dislecksia: The Book, companion to a documentary film.* California: CreateSpace, 2012. (I highly recommend the film.)

Humphries, Susan. *Susan's Story, An autobiographical account of my struggle with dyslexia.* New York: St. Martin's Press, 1982.

International Dyslexia Association (www.interdys.org), Orton Emeritus Series is a group of monographs, each dedicated to a specific topic and written by different experts in the field of dyslexia. Frequently updated.

Jordan, Dale R. *Jordan Dyslexia Assessment/Reading Program, Teacher and Student Manuals,* Pro-ed. (www.proedinc.com), 2000. Dr. Jordan has written several other books on dyslexia and ADHD.

Jordan, Dale R. *Overcoming Dyslexia in Children, Adolescents, and Adults,* 3rd Ed., pro-ed. Austin, Texas, 2002.

Langston, Robert. *The Power of Dyslexic Thinking,* Austin, Texas: Bridgeway Books, 2010.

Lauver, Nelson. *Most UnLikely to Succeed, A Memoir,* New York: Five City Media, 2011.

MacCracken, Mary. *Turnabout Children,* New York: Signet Publishers, 1987.

Moats, Louisa Cook. *Speech to Print: Language Essentials for Teachers,* 2nd Ed., Baltimore, MD: Paul H. Publishing Co., 2010.

Moats, Louisa Cook and Karen E. Dakin, *Basic Facts About Dyslexia and Other Reading Problems,* East Peoria, Ill: The International Dyslexia Association.

Polacco, Patricia. *Thank You, Mr. Falker,* New York: Philomel Books, New York, 1998. (Excellent book to help the child with dyslexia understand himself.)

Porch, Meg and Gilroy, Mary, *Ten in Every Hundred,* Southwest Branch of the International Dyslexia Association, (swida@southwestida.com), 2008. (This short, inexpensive booklet gives basic facts about dyslexia in an easy to read format.)

Pritchard, Heather. *Got Dyslexia?* Mustang, OK: Tate Publishing & Enterprises, 2011. (This is a short child's book with audio download.)

Sargent, Dave. *An Uphill Climb.* Prairie Grove, AR 72753: Ozark Publications, Inc., 1991.

Schmitt, Dr. Abraham as told to Mary Lou Hartzler Clemens. *Brilliant Idiot, An Autobiography of a Dyslexic.* Intercourse, PA: Good Books, January 1, 1994. (This is the heartbreaking story of an older man with dyslexia.)

Schultz, Philip. *MY Dyslexia.* New York: W. W. Norton & Company, Inc., 2011.

Shaywitz, Sally M.D., *Overcoming Dyslexia, A New and Complete Science-Based Program for Reading Problems at Any Level.* New York: Alfred A. Knopf, 2008. (A classic.)

Simpson, E. *Reversals: A Personal Account of Victory Over Dyslexia,* Boston: Houghton Mifflin Co., 1979.

Vail, Priscilla L. *Smart Kids with School Problems. Things to Know and Ways to Help,* New York: Penguin Group, 1989.

Vaz, A. McDonald. *The Doctor who Begged to Be,* Pittsburg, PA: Dorrance Publishing Company, 1995.

West, Thomas G. *In the Mind's Eye: Visual Thinkers, Gifted People With Dyslexia and Other Learning Difficulties, Computer Images and the Ironies of Creativity,* New York: Prometheus Books, 1997.

Winkler, Henry, with Lin Oliver. This is written as a series of seventeen books with Hank Zipzer as the main character. These books show children how to overcome obstacles. Written on a low reading level, children love them. New York: Penguin, Inc. www.hankzipzer.com, 2013.

Wolf, Maryanne. *Proust and the Squid: The story and science of the reading brain.,* New York: Harper Collins, 2007.

Wright, Pam and Peter. *From Emotions to Advocacy,* second edition. Hartfield, VA: Harbor House Law Press, Inc., 2006.

Wright, Pam and Peter. *No Child Left Behind,* Harbor Hartfield, VA: House Law Press, Inc., 2009.

Wright, Pam and Peter. Wrightslaw: *Special Education Law,* 2nd Ed., Hartfield, VA: Harbor House Law Press, Inc., 2006.

Appendix C

Outstanding Persons with Dyslexia

This list is not exhaustive. I have chosen not to include some famous persons reported to have dyslexia. Such persons were deceased prior to establishing accurate assessment procedures. Therefore, we classify these persons as dyslexic from characteristics primarily found in biographies.

Ann E. Bancroft, explorer, lecturer, educator. First woman to travel across the ice to both the North and South Poles

Baruj Benacerraf, M.D., Nobel Prize in Physiology/Medicine

Michael Bennell, U. S. Senator, Colorado

Phil Bryant, governor of Mississippi

George Burns, actor and comedian

Neil Bush, governor of Florida

Stephen J. Cannell, Novelist and Emmy Award-winning writer

Gaston Caperton, former governor of West Virginia

John Chambers, CEO Crisco

Delos M. Cosgrove M. D., chairman of the Department of Thoracic and Cardiovascular Surgery at the Cleveland Clinic

Dom Deluise, actor and comedian

Fannie Flagg, writer and actor most famous for her novel *Fried Green Tomatoes*, which was later made into a movie

Whoopi Goldberg, actor and comedian who has used her stardom to help eliminate homelessness

John R. Horner, technical advisor to Steven Spielberg for *Jurassic Park* and *The Lost World*

Robert Langston, author and speaker

Wendell B. Leimbach Jr., captain, United States Marine Corps

Jay Leno. comedian

Greg E. Louganis, U. S. Olympic gold medalist

Harold Lubin, M.D., psychiatrist

Dan Malloy. governor of Connecticut

Paul J. Orfalea, Businessman, founder of Kinko's

Mike Peters. cartoonist who created *Mother Goose and Grimm*

Nelson Rockefeller, former vice president of the United States

Mic Rodgers, stunt coordinator for feature films, TV and commercials, including *Braveheart, Volcano, and Maverick*

Charles Schwab, financial-services and businessman

Peter E. Shumlin, governor of Vermont

John Skoyles, neuroscientist in evolutionary psychology

Tom Smothers, comedian and showman

Steven Spielberg, film director

Elizabeth Daniels Squire, author of mystery novels

Jackie Stewart, international race car driver

Henry Winkler, actor, producer, director, humanitarian. "Fonz" on ABC-TV's *Happy Days*

Stevie Wonder. musician (attention-deficit disorder)

Peter W. D. Wright, special education attorney

Appendix D

Organizations and Associations

Some groups which may be of help:

Academic Language Therapy Association
www.ALTAread.org

Academy of Orton-Gillingham
Practitioners and Educators
www.ortonacademy.org

ACT Test Administration:
The American College Testing will arrange for
individual administration of assessments for students
with perceptual disabilities, given proper
documentation of the disability.

P. O. Box 4028,
Iowa City, IA 52243
Phone: 319-337-133

ADDitude (magazine)
www.additudemag.com

Alliance for Accreditation and Certification of
Structured Language Education, Inc.
www.allianceaccreditation.org

American Bar Association Child Advocacy &
Protection Center
Phone: 202-662-1000

American Psychological Association
www.apa.org

Association of Educational Therapists
www.aetonline.org

Attention Deficit/ Disorder: Children & Adults with
Attention Deficit/Hyperactivity Disorder (C.H.A.D.D.)
national@chadd.org
Phone: 800-233-4050

British Dyslexia Association
www.bda-dyslexia.org.uk

Center for Early Literacy and Learning
www.earlyliteracylearning.org

Center for Reading and Language Research,
Tufts University
Medford, MA 02155

Children of the Code
www.childrenofthecode.org

Council for Exceptional Children
E-mail cec@cec.sped.org
www.cec.sped.org
Phone: 703-620-3660

Council for Learning Disabilities
www.coe.winthrop.edu/CLD
Phone: 913-492-8755

Council of Parent Attorneys & Advocates (COPPA)
www.edlaw.net

Dyslexia Association of the Pennyrile
www.hopkinsvilledyslexia.org
Phone: 270-885-5804

Dyslexia Research Institute
www.dyslexia-add.org

Dyscalculia
www.unicog.org/docs/Dyscalculia.html

Education Update Online
www.educationupdate.com

Experience Dyslexia,
(Simulation tape that allows one to experience dyslexia)
www.dyslexia-ncbida.org

Financial Aid for Students with Disabilities
www.finaid.org/finaid/documents/heath.html

Florida Center for Reading Research
(resources for scientifically based reading instruction)
www.fcrr.org

Florida organization providing diagnostic testing, academic and tutorial programs, advocacy and adult education
www.floridatechnet.org

For the Children Foundation and the Langston Company, Inc.
www.RobertLangston.com

GED Hotline
(guide for people taking the GED who have learning disabilities)
Phone: 800-629-9433

Great Schools (once Schwab Learning.org)
www.greatschools.net

Haan Foundation for Children
www.haan4kids.org

Home/Learning Disabilities Association of America
www.ldanatl.org
Phone: 412-341- 1515

International Dyslexia Association
(Most states have at least one branch)
www.interdys.org
Phone: 800-222-3123

LD Online
www.ldonline.org

Learning Ally (formerly Recording for the Blind and Dyslexic)
www.LearningAlly.org
Phone: 800-221-4792

National Center on RTI (Response to Intervention)
http://www.rti4success.org

National Council on Teacher Quality, research & advocacy group that focuses on quality teaching
www.nctq.org

National Institute of Child Health and Human Development
www.nichd.nih.gov/

National Institute for Learning Disabilities
NILD
www.nild.org

National Institute of Mental Health
http://www.nimh.nih.gov
Phone: 888-615-6464

National Institute of Neurological Disorders
www.ninds.nih.gov/disorders/dyslexia.html

Neuhaus Center
www.neuhaus.org
Phone: 281-664-7676

Slingerland Institute for Literacy
www.slingerland.org
Phone: 425-453-1190

United States Department of Education
www.ed.gov

United States Department of Education's Office of
Special Education and Rehabilitative Services (OSERS)
www.idea.ed.gov

Wrights Law
www.wrightslaw.com

Yale Center for Dyslexia and Creativity
www.dyslexia.yale.edu

About the Author

The author grew up on a Kentucky farm and currently lives in Western Kentucky. She borrowed  money and worked two jobs to complete an undergraduate degree with honors at Austin Peay State University, Clarksville, TN. She earned a master's degree in elementary education from George Peabody College of Vanderbilt University and a second masters in psychology from Austin Peay University.

Ms. Lature taught thirty-five years in public school systems, where she quickly developed a passion for students with reading disabilities. At a time when persons with dyslexia were grossly misunderstood, Ms. Lature took advantage of the sparse opportunities to become trained in multisensory education. As she continued to work in public education, she helped organized a low-cost community program—Dyslexia

Association of the Pennyrile. After forty-two years, she continues to serve as its executive director.

Besides dyslexia, her present interests are antique glassware and travel in both the United States and abroad. She has been to several European countries, Central America, and the Middle East.

Ms. Lature has been an adjunct professor at Hopkinsville Community College and Murray State University. She has spoken at Title I state conferences, regional IRA conferences, and for the dyslexia association. Ms. Lature also does dyslexia workshops for associations, schools, and civic groups.

You can e-mail Ruth at lature1445@aol.com or visit her website at www.ruthlature.com.

Endnotes

[1] Peabody Picture Vocabulary Test is an untimed test given orally to provide an estimate of verbal intelligence.

[2] Dolch Basic Sight Words were originally chosen by Edward Dolch and published in 1948. Many of these two-hundred twenty words cannot be sounded out and must be remembered by sight. These words are the most common words encountered in children's books.

[3] Phonology is a study of the smallest unit of speech that distinguishes one word from another. *Cat* has three phonemes: *k*, *a*, and *t*.

[4] Syntax is the way in which words are put together to form phrases, clauses, and sentences.

[5] Morphology is the study of meaningful linguistic units that have no smaller parts. This would include prefixes and suffixes, root words, as well as their functional use and spelling patterns.

[6] The look-say method studies words and remembers them by their configuration or their look.

[7] *Fact Sheet, What is Dyslexia?* (International Dyslexia Association), www.interdys.org.

[8] Datuk Shahrizat and Seri Shahrizat, *Early Dyslexia Detection Programmes in all Nurseries* (The Star Online, Feb.14, 2012), http://thestar.com.

[9] *Just the Facts…Attention-Deficit/Hyperactive Disorder (AD/HD) and Dyslexia,* International Dyslexia Association, (May 2008). www.interdys.org

[10] Nancy Mather, *Is It ADHD or Dyslexia – or Both?* (Everyday Health, Inc., 2011).

[11] Executive function is a term for cognitive processes that regulate and control activities such as planning, working memory, and attention.

[12] *DSM: Diagnostic and Statistical Manual of the American Psychiatric Association* is a manual published by the American Psychiatric Association that includes all currently recognized mental-health disorders.

[13] Maia Szalavitz, *These Are Not Gateway Drugs (New York Times,* June 9, 2012). Ms. Szalavitz is a neuroscience journalist for Time.com.

[14] Sandy Newmark, "The ADHD Food Fix: How to Fight ADHD Symptoms With Diet and Supplements," (Winter, 2011). www.ADDitudeMag.com.

[15] Stanford-Binet Intelligence Scale is a standardized test that measures intelligence in children and adults from age two through mature adulthood. It is individually administered, usually by a psychologist.

[16] Slosson Intelligence Test provides a quick, reliable index of intellectual ability for ages 4-65.

[17] IQ represents Intelligence Quotient. It is derived from one of several standardized tests. IQ scores are used as predictors of educational achievement, special needs, and job achievement. IQ was once thought of as mainly inherited.

However, we now know that other factors play a significant role in one's IQ.

[18] Gilmore Oral Reading Test is designed to measure performance in oral-reading accuracy, comprehension, and rate of reading for pupils in grades one through eight. The test consists of paragraphs of increasing difficulty.

[19] Dr. Gordon Sherman has been a leader in the field of dyslexia for thirty years. Former director of the research lab at Beth Israel Deaconess Medical Center in Boston and former faculty member at Harvard Medical School, he is currently at The Newgrange School in Hamelton, N. J., a private school for children with disabilities

[20] Dr. Kenneth Pugh is an associate professor in Pediatrics at the Yale School of Medicine and one of the first to use fMRIs to reveal activity associated with reading and reading disabilities.

[21] Dr. Maryanne Wolf is director of the Center for Reading and Language Research at Tufts University.

[22] We began in 1970 as an affiliate of the Kentucky Association for Specific-Perceptual Motor Disability, Louisville, KY..

[23] Carol Anne Blitzer, "Gibson Honored for Dyslexia Work," (Capital City Press LLC, 7290 Bluebonnet, Blvd., Baton Rouge, LA 70810, 2011).

[24] Hyperkinesis: In 1970, Dr. Shedd was using this term for what we now consider as ADHD or ADD.

---

[25] Marcia K. Henry and Susan G Brickley, eds., *Dyslexia…Samuel T. Orton and His Legacy,* (The International Dyslexia Association, 1999).

[26] Marcia K. Henry. Orton and Gillingham: <u>Legend, Lore, and Legacy,</u> (speech at The International Dyslexia Association Conference, November 9-12, 2011, Chicago, Illinois).

[27] APSL: stood for Alphabetic-Phonetic-Structural-Linguistic, which was the name of Dr.Shedd's method.

[28] IMSLEC: The International Multisensory Structured Language Education Council, 1995, 13140 Coit Road, Suite 320, LB 120, Dallas, TX 75240

[29] SPMD: short for Specific-Perceptual Motor Disability.

[30] Betsy Bond, past president of Dyslexia Association of the Pennyrile, (Association newsletter).

[31] Reading at first grade, third month level.

[32] Section 504 is a civil rights statue that protects all persons from discrimination on the basis of disability (Rehabilitation Act of 1973). Students may be granted extended time, a quiet work environment, a scribe, or other accommodation.

[33] Individuals with Disability Education Act: IDEA—is a federal law that governs how states and public agencies provide early intervention, special education, and related services to children with disabilities.

[34] Shannon Kennedy, <u>Police Handcuff Georgia Kindergartner for Tantrum;</u> Kentucky *New Era,* April 18, 2012.

[35] Lauver, Nelson. *Most Unlikely to Succeed*, (Five City Media Press, 2011).

[36] Dennis O'Neal, New Discipline Rule Worries Schools (*Kentucky New Era,* October 25, 2012).

[37] Merrill Linguistic Readers are decodable textbooks. Each book covers specific phonetic skill as well as sight works. For example, the first book in the series deals with short "*a*", consonants, and a few easy sight words. New sounds are gradually introduced. These books are recommended for grades K-6 but can be used with any student needing a particular decoding skill. Linguistic readers have no pictures. Comprehension is acquired through the printed word.

[38] Controlled-vocabulary: Words are introduced according to a sequence. Usually this sequence is consonants, short vowels, consonant digraphs, consonant blends, long vowels in one syllable words, etc.

[39]Decode: The ability to sound out letters and words.

[40] Reading series: A basal reading program that uses textbooks to guide the teaching of reading strategies. Usually a textbook company develops reading books on different levels and supplementary materials.

[41]Psychometrists: Professionals who administers and scores psychological and neuropsychological tests.

[42] ARC—Admissions and Release Committee is a team of individuals responsible for developing, reviewing, and/or revising an Individual Education Program (IEP) for a child

with a disability. A Federal mandate lists team members who must be present: parent or guardian, teacher(s), school representatives, and an individual who can interpret tests results.

[43] Discrepancy Formula: Method for determining whether a student qualifies for special education through the difference in intelligence and achievement tests. Each state established its own formulate (number of points between IQ and achievement). The Individual Disability Education Act signed into law in 2004 does not require states to use the discrepancy formula.

[44] Individual Education Program (IEP) A written statement for each child with a disability that is developed, reviewed, and revised. A list of requirements to be included is laid out in Sections 300.320 – 300.324 of IDEA.

[45] Sally Shaywitz, M.D., *Overcoming Dyslexia;* (Alfred A. Knopf, New York, 2003).

[46] Basal: Many standardized tests precede along a continuum from easy to difficult for their age group. In an appropriate test, a student should know some of the easier items but gradually know fewer and fewer answers until he misses a designated number. The basal is established when a student starts to miss easier items.

[47] Gabrielle E Anderson, and others, <u>Grade Retention, Achievement and Mental Health Outcomes</u> (National Association of School Psychologists, October 2002).

[48] Brock L. Eide, M. D., and Fernette F, Eide, M.D., *The Dyslexic Advantage*, 1st Ed. (New York: Hudson Street Press, First Printing 2011).

[49] *Associated Press,* Bryant Signs Laws Affecting Students and Veterans (*Washington Examiner*, May 23, 2012). http://washingtonexaminer.com/entertainment/health/2012/0 5/bryant-signs-laws-affecting.

[50] Ted Mann, Governor's Childhood Filled with Obstacles to Overcome, (*Connecticut Post*, Dec. 7, 2011). (http://www.ctpost.com/local/article/Governor-s-childhood-filled-with-obstacles-to 235581).

[51] James F. Russell, Vermont Gov. Peter E. Shumlin tells Eagle Hill Grads to Embrace Non-Traditional Learning, (Worcester Telegram and Gazette Corp, 2012).

[52] Harold Lubin, Your Questions Answered…, (*Perspectives,* Vol. 20, No. 1, winter, 1994).

[53] Sally Shaywitz, M.D., *Overcoming Dyslexia,* (New York: Alfred A. Knopf, New York, 2003).

[54] WBEZ91.5, Chicago, "The Cost of Literacy: Overcoming Learning Disabilities," (June 1, 2012.), (http://www.wbez.org/series/front-center/cost-literacy-overcoming-learning-disabilities-99297).

[55] Grover Whitehurst. "Report on Literacy Program," (MA: Eric B. Easton Publisher).

[56] Public Law 94-142: Law passed in 1975 that states in order to receive federal funds, states must develop and implement assurances that a free appropriate public education will be provided to all children with disabilities. This included the word dyslexia.

[57]Shedd Academy: a private school in Mayfield, KY, for persons with learning differences, which has now closed.

[58] Bill Bartlemanl; *Graves Mom Stresses Dyslexic Students' Needs*, (*The Paducah Sun*, March 1, 2006).

[59] Tanya Rose; <u>Suicide Victim Joey Ferrara Had Been Ready for a Fresh Start</u>, (*PleasantonPatch,*Ca), (Autumn.Johnson@patch.com).

[60] Dyslexia and Youth Suicide, www.dyslexicsuicide.com.

[61] Editorial Staff, <u>Glossary of Early Learning and Literacy Terms,</u> (NCLD, March 11, 2009),(http://www.ncld.org).

[62] Ibid.

[63] National Council of Learning Disabilities. NCLD.org.

[64] Jay Mathews, <u>Our Ignorance of Learning Disabilities</u>; *Washington Post*, (www.washingtonpost.org), (September 2, 2012). A survey done by National Center for Learning Disabilities.

[65] Ibid.

[66] Sylvester, Harry. *Legacy of the Blue Heron,* Oxton House Publishers; 2006.

[67] National Institute of Child Health and Human Development, Rockville, MD www.nichd.nih.gov

[68] National Institute for Literacy, www.caliteracy.org

[69] *Adult Literacy Programs,* Literacy Partners, Inc., www.literacypartners.org.

[70] Michael Hayes, "Just the Facts," compiled for The (International Dyslexia Association from U.S. Department of Education).

[71] Kathryn Currier Moody. *Dyslexia in the Prison Population, 2000,* (www.educationupdate.com/archives/2008DEC/html/spec--dyslexia.html).

[72] Jessica Fletcher, *"Kentucky Chamber*: Skyrocketing Inmate Cost Hurt School Funding," (Kentucky Chamber of Commerce, 2009).

[73] National Longitudinal Transition Study, (1994: 23rd Annual Report to Congress, 2001).

[74] Pete Stark and Bill Cassidy. "Stark and Cassidy: Dyslexia is Bipartisan Issue with Solutions,"(*Dyslexia Action,* May 2012),(http://www.rollcall.com/issues/57_136/Pete_Stark_Bill_Cassidy_Dyslexia_Bipartisanissue).

[75] Individuals with Disabilities Education Act: 2004. (http://www.ldonline.org/features/idea2004).

[76] Texas 2009: HB 461 *Regulations of Dyslexia Practitioners.* (http://www.statutes.legis.state.tx.us).

23097689R00169

Made in the USA
Charleston, SC
11 October 2013